TINA:
An Autobiography
with Genealogy

by
Justina E. Smith

BROADBLADE PRESS
11314 Miller Road
Swartz Creek, MI 40473

Copyright 1988 by Robert N. and Victor H. Smith, Jr.

ISBN 0–9620249–1–0 (casebound)
ISBN 0–9620249–0–2 (perfect bound)

Typeset by Sans Serif, Inc., Ann Arbor, Michigan
Printed by McNaughton & Gunn, Saline, Michigan

I would like to dedicate this book to my wonderful
family, especially to the memory of my deceased son,
Vernon, and to my sons Robert and Victor, Jr.,
and their wives, with love and devotion.

I must express my deep appreciation and gratitude to
Jeanette Dahlgren for her assistance and untiring
dedication in organizing and typing the material.
Without her, this book could never have been written.

CONTENTS

ILLUSTRATIONS

ACKNOWLEDGEMENTS

Albert Beers

Brian and Cindy Brandt

Jeanette L. Dahlgren

Bessie Johnson Delanoy

Norman Hollis Duke

Myrtle E. Elie

Edna H. Mitchell

Virginia Sparkman

Briarwood Manor Nursing Home
Aids
Nurses
Staff

Calvert Park Church of God
The Keenagers

First Pilgrim Holiness Church
Rev. J.C. Brillhart
Rev. A.C. Doehring
Rev. A.S. Joppie
Rev. W.N. Miller
Rev. B.O. Shattuck
Rev. L.W. Sturk

First Wesleyan Church
Rev. D. Wayne Brown
Rev. Jay DeNeff
Rev. R.B. Webster

CHAPTER I

MY GOALS AND OUR FAMILY TREE

FOR YEARS I have possessed a driving ambition to write my life story. During my active middle years I could not find time to get at this personal assignment. It is just as well, for it would have been incomplete if written at that time.

Now, at ninety-seven, I have time and realize that there will not be much more to add or accomplish except my desire. That is, and always has been, to live to be one hundred years old.

Because I am legally blind and my hearing is considerably below normal, interruptions of my line of thought are few. Thus, concentration on the subject has been effortless and quite complete. Currently, my most valuable asset is my mentality with which I have been endowed. It is all powerful through the gift of God and enables me to remember and even recall bits of information from the recesses of my memory after dwelling on them intensely for various short periods of time.

A few roots of this autobiography must be exposed to the public so that the "how come" will be understandable. An important decision was made by my parents which proved to be the determining factor of my life. Likewise, things which I have done will plot the course of those who will follow me in lineage strung out even to what used to be called "shirt-tail" relatives. Also, decisions made earlier in life by people who have preceded me as to living standards, desire for education and physical location have a bearing on the life direction of close friends. I have lived long enough to observe this taking place.

In earlier days, even several decades before the Gold Rush, there was a great migration from the East to claim homesteads or buy more fertile land farther to the West. Two families, not related and previously unknown to each other, took up adjacent land in a section of the Northwest Territory. This portion became the State of Michigan in 1837. They were the Sages and the Whites. It was a coincidence that each family had three girls and four boys.

I should like to put the second root down right here. It is important enough to be compared to the tap root of a tree. It is heritage. My contribution to these two families and the descendants thereof is the genealogical information which follows on the next few pages. I have recorded much of it as the years have spun rapidly by. Oh! They go so fast. Earlier portions were tied down only after diligent research coupled with sometimes lengthy correspondence. In other instances patience has been the word and I am still awaiting bits of vital information at the time that this documentation is being made for me by Jeanette Dahlgren. You will note several omissions which I have been unable to fill in because I was unsuccessful in tracking down the information needed or to substantiate that already available.

At various times, as the word went out that I had this family tree, many of the Sage, White, Valentine and Root families or those who had married into these families have querried me about kinfolks or asked to view my original charts. So here they are in their entirety for all to have and to use. It has been necessary to do some cutting and piecing to place them on the pages of this book. It is possible that they may be considered more valuable and examined with more diligence by generations yet to come.

It is my prayer that a few copies of this autobiography containing, among other things, this genealogy will be preserved for use by posterity.

GEORGE AND HANNAH (BRONSON) WHITE

George and Hannah (Bronson) White both born during the administration of our first President in the 1790s. They had nine children and are the great-great-great-grandparents of my boys.

GRANDPA ALPHEUS, AND GRANDMA WHITE 1819–1883

Samantha (Root) 1826–1919 was married at sixteen.

GRANDPA AND GRANDMA SAGE

Henry D., 1829–1926 and Justina (Valentine), 1836–1918. The photograph was taken at East Jordan, Michigan where Uncle Clayton, an artist, lived.

HENRY D. SAGE
HEADSTONE

Sage headstone in Mt. Hope Cemetery on Cook Road, a bit west of Jennings Road, one mile south of Rankin, Michigan.

FAMILY OF HENRY D. AND JUSTINA (VALENTINE) SAGE, JULY, 1885

Left to right, Top: William H., age 20; Harriet, age 25; and Frank M., age 25. Left to right, Center: Esther Ann, 27; Henry D., age 56; Justina, age 49; and Janet D., age 29. Left to right, Boys: Fred Judson, age 14; Freddie, age 3; and Clayton, age 9. The photograph was taken in Flint on Henry's birthday.

FAMILY OF REV. NATHAN IRA AND ESTHER ANN (SAGE) WHITE, NOVEMBER, 1909

Left to right, Top: Mildred E., age 16; Grace E., age 20; and Justine E., age 18. Left to right, Bottom: Ruth E., age 9; Rev. Nathan, age 51; E. Ann, age 51; and Mary E., age 13. At this time Pa was minister in three churches, West Branch, Campbells Corners and Edwards. I was teaching country school at East Twining. We were all proud of Pa.

OUR FAMILY TREE

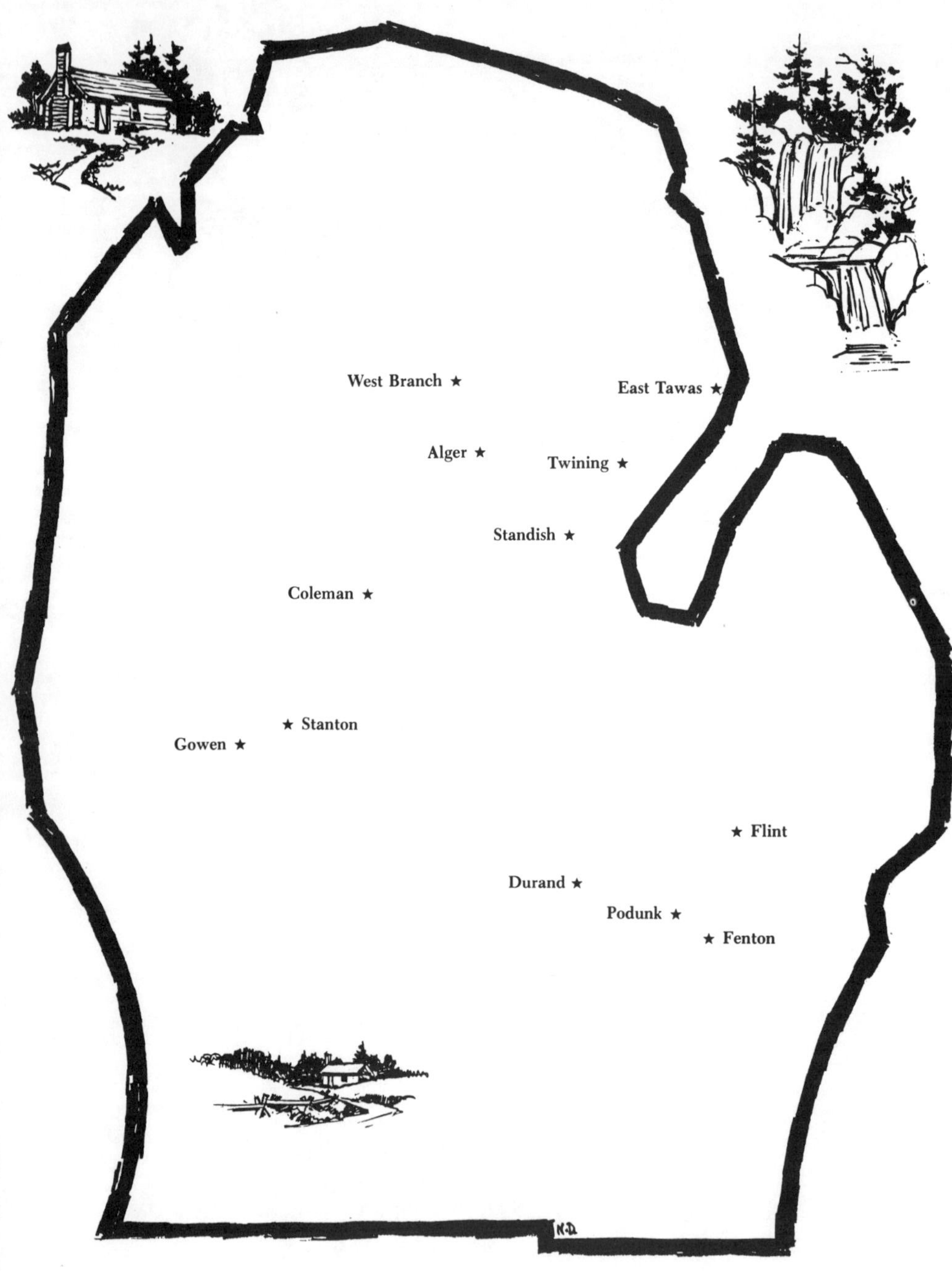

Places where I lived during my lifetime of meandering Michigan.

SAGE GENEALOGY
1639 – 1971

Scandinavian Origin

Words engraved on Saga coat of arms – "Non Sibi," — meaning "Not for Ourselves."

Drawn by Justina Smith. 7th generation from David. Oct. 1st, 1971 from original authentic sketch found in the front of book published in 1878 by Elisha Sage, from authentic records of the descendants of David Sage. This coat of arms was granted the Sages in England, by William the Conqueror in 1066.

From Sage Genealogical Book, page 13 – The Sage family numbers in its ranks, persons in all avocations of life – judges, lawyers, clergymen, doctors of divinity, professors in colleges, teachers, medical doctors, military and naval officers, state senators, representatives, members of Congress, merchants, manufacturers and mechanics – but a very great majority follow agricultural pursuits. They are true to their motto on the family coat of arms – "Non Sibi", not for ourselves.

David Sage
b. 1639 [1]

d. 1703

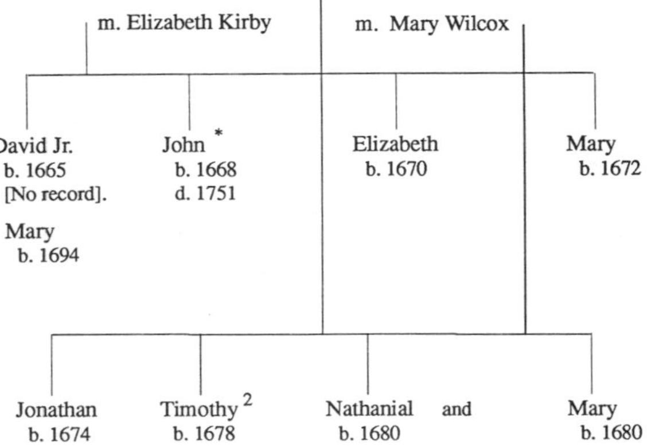

m. Elizabeth Kirby   m. Mary Wilcox

David Jr.
b. 1665
[No record].

John *
b. 1668
d. 1751

Elizabeth
b. 1670

Mary
b. 1672

Mary
b. 1694

Jonathan
b. 1674

Timothy [2]
b. 1678

Nathanial and
b. 1680

Mary
b. 1680

* Continued on own page.
[1] Came from Wales, age 13.
[2] His son, Amos –1722– was great grandfather of Elisha Sage, 1889, author of Sage book.

Original name Saga – Later Le Sage

The Sage family settled near Middletown, Conn., 1652 – original name of town—Matabeset (Indian). Buried near Middletown in Riverside Cemetery at N. end of Main St. Descendants still there – also near Cromwell Conn. Many are farmers – as was David. This land is in the N.E. part of the present town of Cromwell, Conn., along the banks of the Connecticut River.

Compiled Sept. 10, 1971 by Justina Eliza White Smith from writings my mother – Esther Ann Sage left and also from the Sage Book written by Elisha L. Sage, great great great grandson of David. Records can still be found in the State Library at Hartford, Conn. The coat of arms was brought from London by Capt. Nathan Sage shortly after the War of Independence and was given to his daughter, Mrs. Norman Knox, wife of a former pres. of Hartford Bank. Her adopted daughter wrought a facsimile of the design in silk – which is still perserved.

A FEW SAGE NOTABLES:

Capt. Nathan Sage – 1752 – in the navy – captured a British vessel loaded with powder needed by American forces. Was admitted to Congress. Later was a famous judge.

Rufus B. Sage – author of "Scenes in the Rocky Mts." – a warrior against hostile Indians.

Phinias Sage – a prominent M.D. in colonial times and later.

Russel Sage – 1816 – millionaire and noted philanthropist and benefactor.

Capt. David Sage, grandson of David, a noted leader during pre-Revolutionary War days.

Rev. Charles H. Sage, Free Methodist minister and author.

Carlton L. Sage – 1822 – Bearer of Dispatches to foreign countries during Pres. Millard Fillmore's administration. He was brother of our Grandpa Sage.

William Sage – 1748– fought at Bunker Hill.

Philander Sage — Senator in Indiana.

Miles Sage — 1785 and Sparrow Sage — 1781 — cited for great bravery in the War for Independence.

Col. Hezekiah Sage — 1790 — Sageville, N.Y. named for him.

Comfort Sage was Colonel in the Revolutionary War.

SAGE GENEALOGY

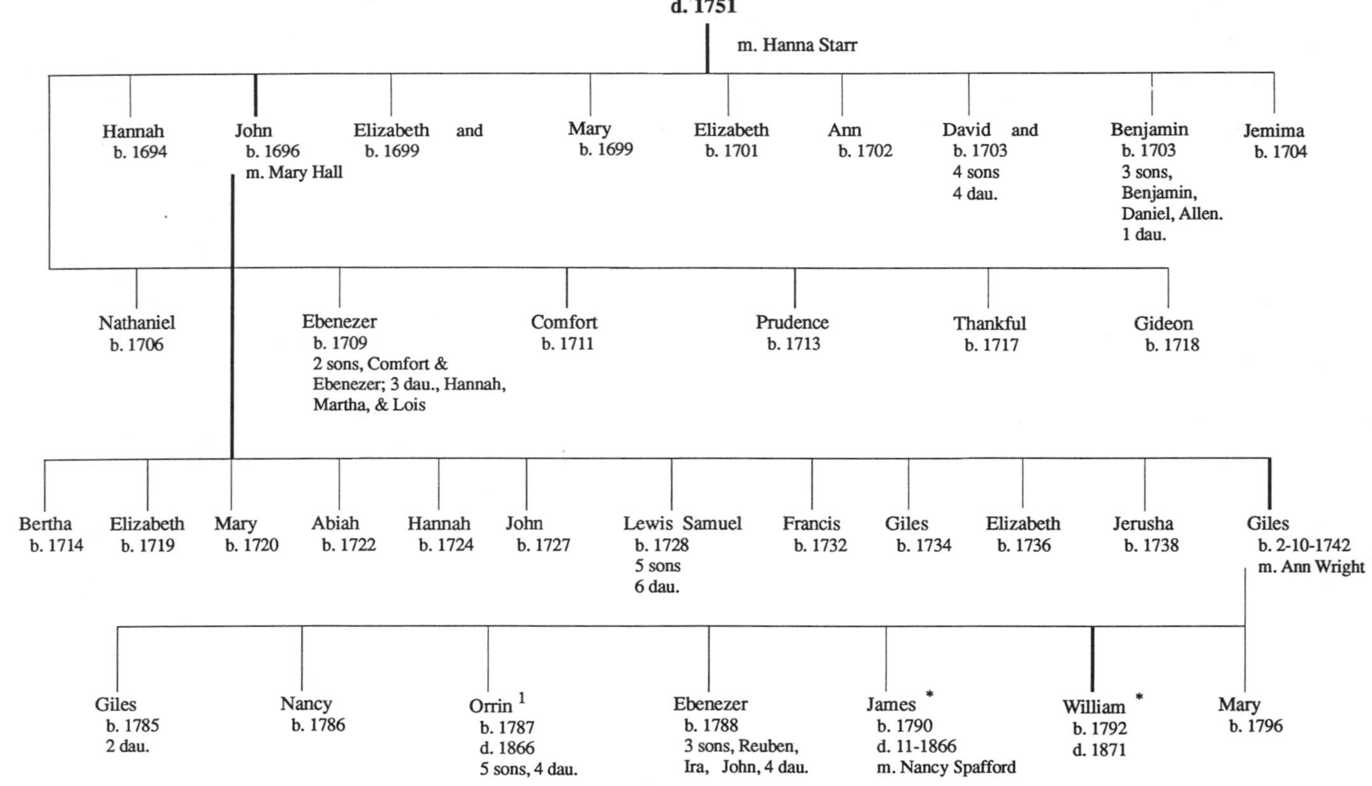

* Continued on own page.
1 A merchant in Rochester, N.Y.

SAGE GENEALOGY

James Sage
b. 1790
d. 11-1866

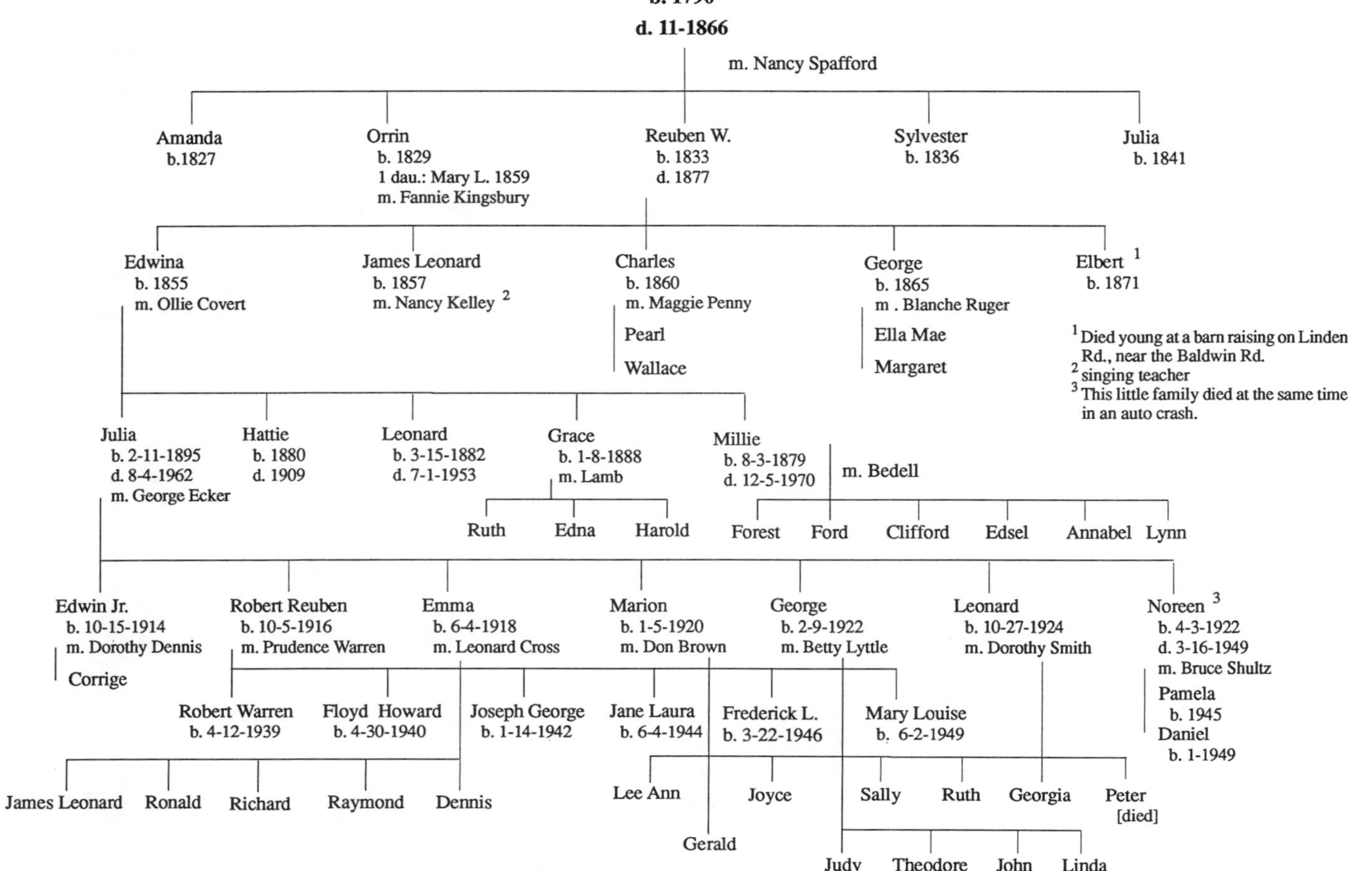

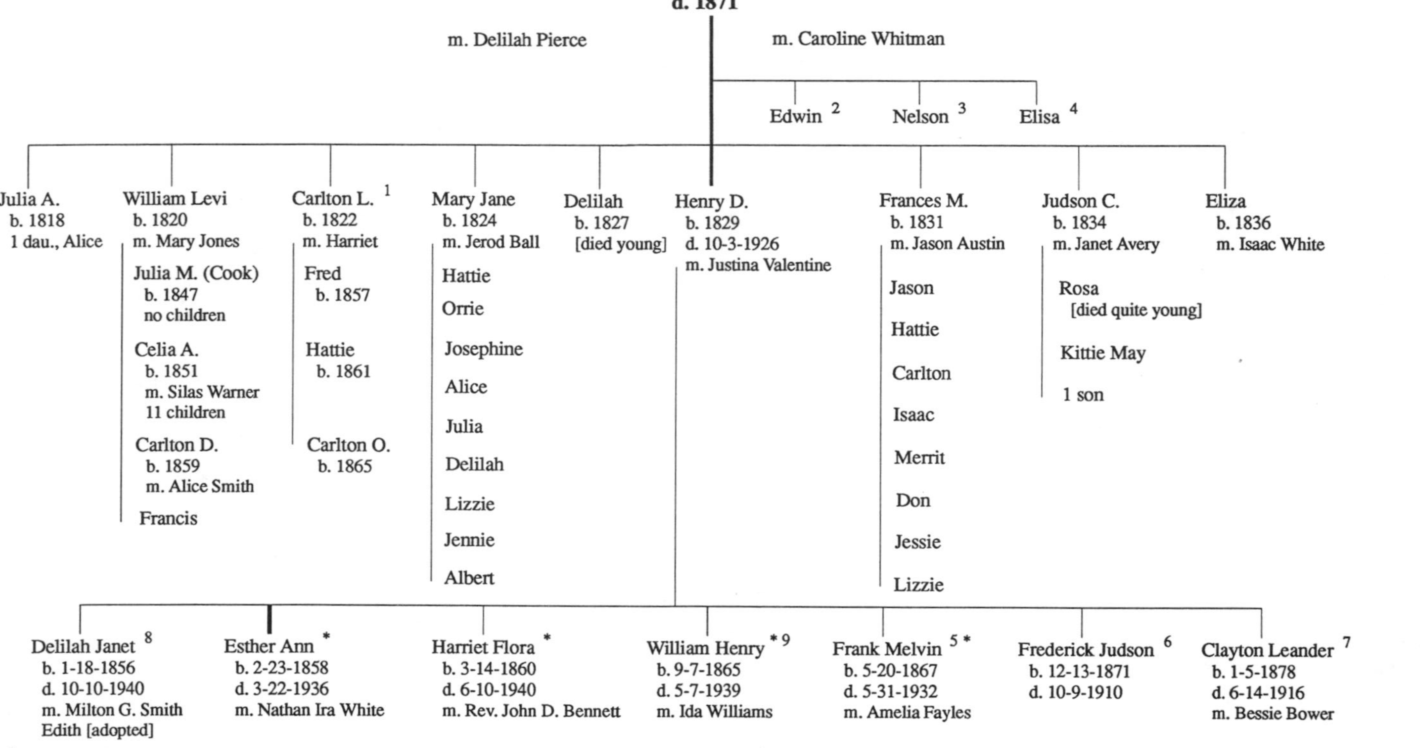

* Continued on own page.
1 Carlton L. was ambassador to Europe under Pres. M. Fillmore
2 Lived for a time with his sister, Eliza and husband – Uncle Ike. One son in Salvation Army – Wash. D.C.
3 Died in early life in a R.R. accident. Left a wife and small daughter, Norma.
4 Cannot find these dates.
5 Born on a farm near Midland – later moved to Freeland, Mich. where he continued farming.
6 Never married. Worked on his Dad's farm, at Mundy, Mich. on the Linden Road. We called him Uncle Jud.
7 He was an artist, and worked at sign painting in Needles, Cal. On June 14, 1916, a man, dissatisfied over delay in getting some signs finished, struck him a severe blow in the head and he died that day. No children.
8. No children. Lived at N. Bradley, Mich. Adopted Edith. Married Vern Childs.
9 Farmer.

SAGE/VALENTINE GENEALOGY

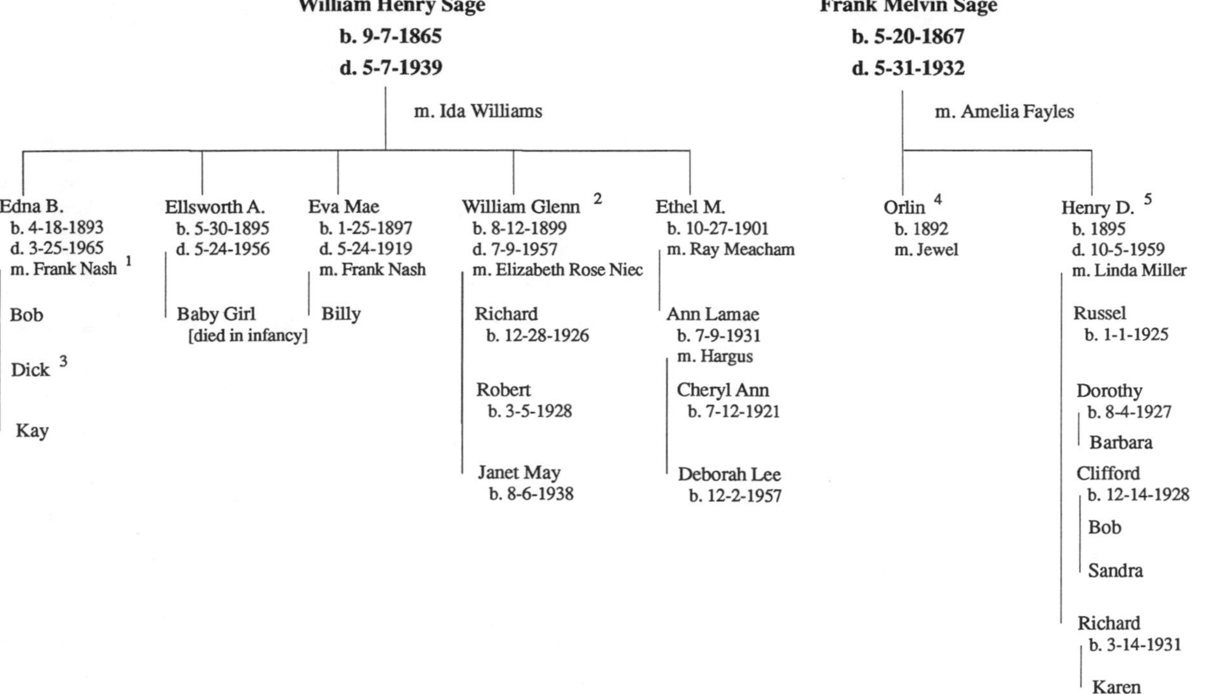

William Henry Sage
b. 9-7-1865
d. 5-7-1939

m. Ida Williams

Frank Melvin Sage
b. 5-20-1867
d. 5-31-1932

m. Amelia Fayles

Edna B.
b. 4-18-1893
d. 3-25-1965
m. Frank Nash [1]

Bob

Dick [3]

Kay

Ellsworth A.
b. 5-30-1895
d. 5-24-1956

Baby Girl
[died in infancy]

Eva Mae
b. 1-25-1897
d. 5-24-1919
m. Frank Nash

Billy

William Glenn [2]
b. 8-12-1899
d. 7-9-1957
m. Elizabeth Rose Niec

Richard
b. 12-28-1926

Robert
b. 3-5-1928

Janet May
b. 8-6-1938

Ethel M.
b. 10-27-1901
m. Ray Meacham

Ann Lamae
b. 7-9-1931
m. Hargus

Cheryl Ann
b. 7-12-1921

Deborah Lee
b. 12-2-1957

Orlin [4]
b. 1892
m. Jewel

Henry D. [5]
b. 1895
d. 10-5-1959
m. Linda Miller

Russel
b. 1-1-1925

Dorothy
b. 8-4-1927

Barbara

Clifford
b. 12-14-1928

Bob

Sandra

Richard
b. 3-14-1931

Karen

[1] Edna married Frank Nash after Eva died, and raised Billy
[2] Lived at Swartz Creek.
[3] The Nash Brothers – with their dad, Frank – run a hardware store in Battle Creek, Mi.
[4] Born on a farm. Later a commercial fisherman on Lake Superior at Superior, Wisconsin. Retired to Bonita Springs, Florida.
[5] Born on a farm – later lived and worked at Detroit, Mich.

SAGE/VALENTINE GENEALOGY

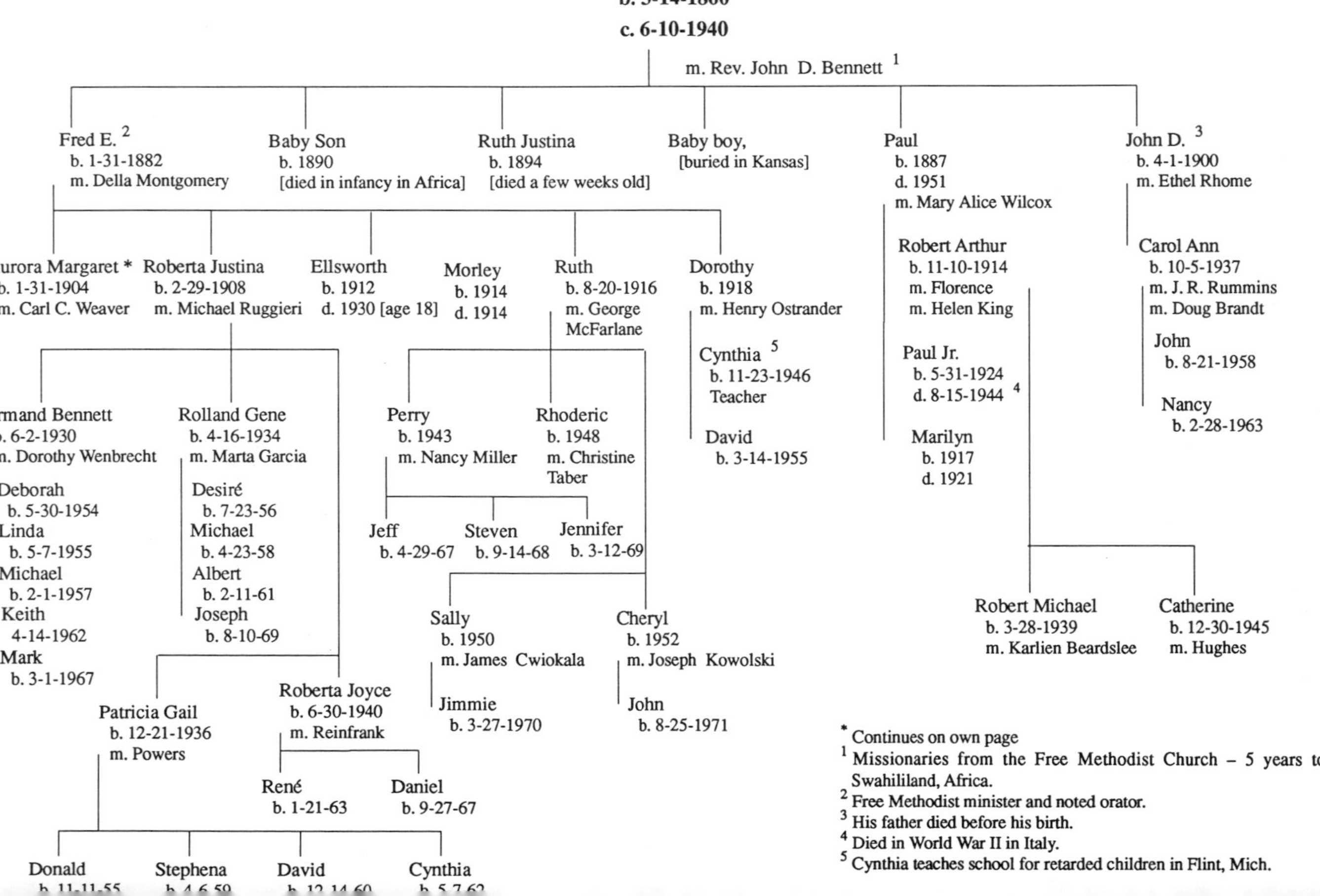

WHITE/SAGE GENEALOGY

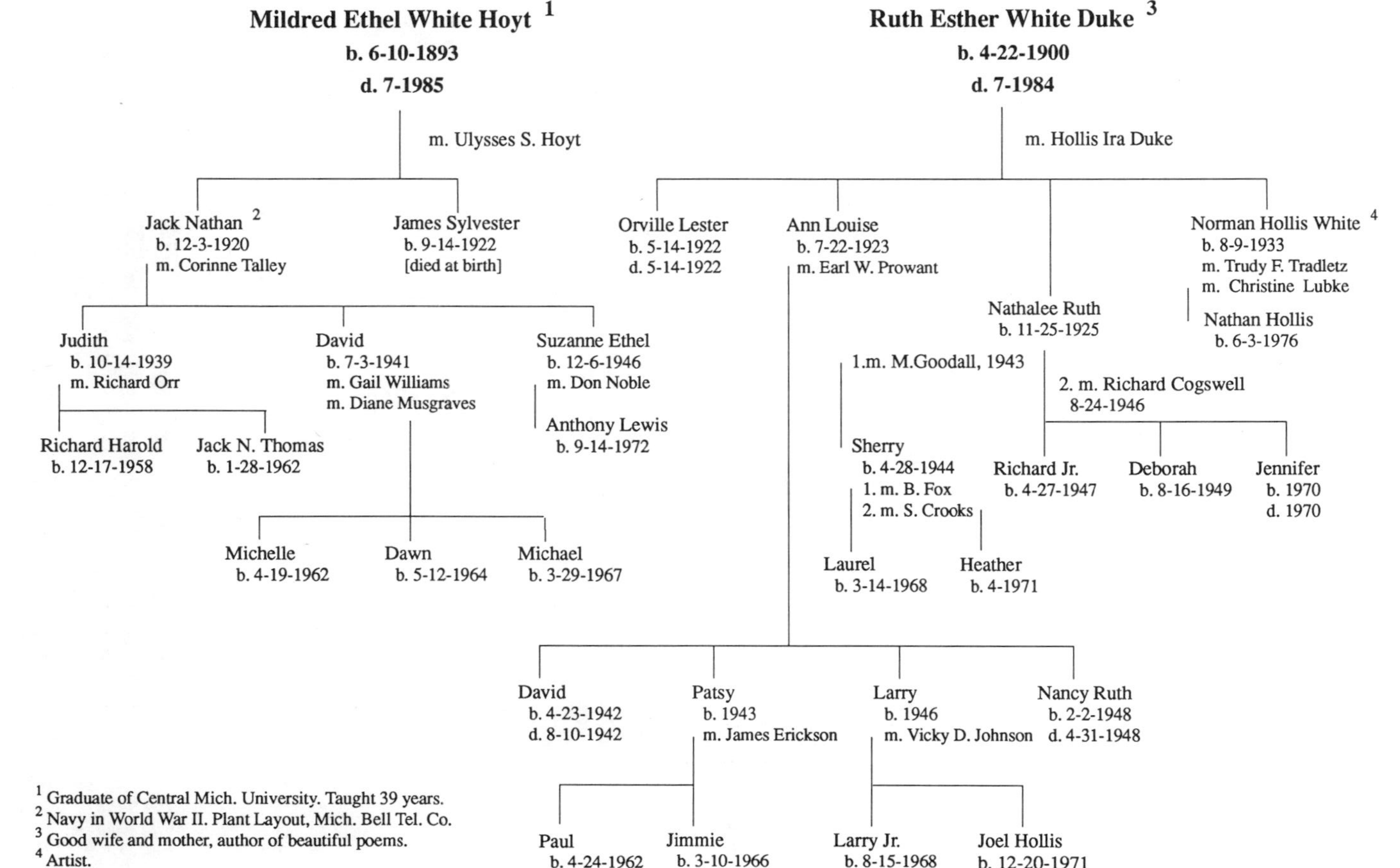

VALENTINE GENEALOGY
1750 —1971

Grandma — Justina Valentine Sage's Family

Jacob Valentine —— Justina S. Tuller

married about 1750

Direct Line starts with Prince Wolfert Webber of Holland [1664] as follows, to clarify the line down to the first Valentine – Jacob [about 1750.]
1. Wolfert Webber – Prince of Holland
2. Aneka Jans (his daughter) m. Bogardus
3. Sarah (1st child of Aneka) m. Kersted.
4. Rachael (second child of Sarah Kersted) m. Tuller.
5. Jacobus (4th child of Rachael Tuller) m. ?
6. Justina (7th child of Jacobus) Tuller m. Jacob Valentine.
7. John Valentine – son of Jacob & Justina (Tuller) m. Sarah Truesdale
8. Cornelius (4th child of John & Sarah) m. Esther Alger.
9. Justina (4th child of Cornelius & Esther) m. Henry D. Sage.

It is plain to see that my given name, Justina, came from Holland – and first appears – Justina Tuller – who was the 7th child of Jacobus Tuller, and Jacobus was the great, great grandson of Prince Wolfert Webber, so the first Justina was a great, great, great — of the Prince. Also, this Justina Tuller Valentine was the great grandmother of my grandma, Justina Valentine Sage – for whom I – Justina E. White Smith, was named. The name Justina appears in several other descendants as seen by this genealogy – down to my granddaughter Justine Ann Smith.

Son John, — probably other children too.

John Valentine, age 22 —— Sarah Truesdale, age 19

married — June 10, 1793

b. 5-4-1771 b. 6-10-1793
d. ? d. 4-11-1844

John	James	Justina	Cornelius	Huldah	Louise	Orilla	Arora	Nancy	William
b. 1794	b. 1795	b. 1797	b. 1-19-1800	b. 1804	b. 1806	b. 1808	b. 1810	b. 1815	b. 1823
			d. 1-16-1855						
			m. Esther Alger [1]						
			12-13-1827						

Martha	Andrew	Mary	Justina [*]	Josiah	Ursula	Esther	Sarah Jane
b. 12-5-1829	b. 4-8-1831	b. 8-31-1833	b. 6-21-1836	b. 9-16-1838	b. 1-19-1842	b. 10-4-1845	b. 3-19-1848
d. 11-12-1860	d. 1-5-1908	d. 2-15-1848	d. 1-25-1918	d. 7-21-1922	d. 9-23-1881	d. 11-3-1921	d. 10-24-1926
m. Myron Whitmore	m. Adelia Demund	[age 14]	m. Henry D. Sage	m. Nancy Hemstead	m. William Bloss	m. Harris Odell	m. George Turner
[blind]							
	Eva			Justina	Effie	George	Leon
	m. Bedell				m. Wilcox		
	Mina			James	Matie	Charles	Katie
	m. Woodthorpe						m. Bigelow
	Fannie			Jennie	Jasper	Beatrice	Willie
	M. Teneate					m. Crane	
	[blind]						
						Myrtie	
						m. Ormiston	
						m. Beamis	
						Elmer	

* Continues on own page
[1] Esther was the daughter of Esther and Josiah Alger, M.D. She and Cornelius moved by oxen to Troy in Genesee County, July, 1836. He gave ground for cemetery "Mt. Hope" in Genesee Co., Mich..

VALENTINE GENEALOGY

Justina Valentine Sage
b. 6-21-1836
d. 1-25-1918

m. Henry D. Sage

Delilah Janet
b. 6-18-1856
d. 10-10-1940
m. Milton Smith
Edith [adopted].

Esther Ann [*]
b. 2-23-1858
d. 3-1936
m. Nathan Ira White

Harriet Flora [*]
b. 3-14-1860
d. 6-10-1940
m. Rev. John D. Benett
1 son [died in infancy]

William Henry
b. 4-7-1865
d. 4-7-1939
m. Ida Williams

Frank Melvin
b. 5-20-1867
d. 5-31-1932
m. Amelia Fails

Judson Frederick
b. 12-13-1870
d. 10-1-1910

Clayton Leander [1]
b. 1-5-1878
d. 6-16-1916
m. Bess Bowan

Children of William Henry

Edna B.
b. 7-13-1893
d. 3-25-1965
m. Frank Nash

Bob

Dick

Kay

Billy [4]

Ellsworth
b. 4-3-1895
d. 4-12-1956

Baby
b. 1909
[died in infancy]

Eva Mae
b. 1-20-1892
d. 3-24-1919
m. Frank Nast

Billy [4]

William Glen
b. 8-20-1899
d. 9-18-1957
m. Betty Nier

Richard Glen
b. 12-28-1926

Robert Dean
b. 3-5-1928

Janet May
b. 8-6-1938

Ethel
b. 10-27-1901
m. R. Meacham

Ann Lamae
m. Hargus

Cheryl Ann
b. 7-12-1951

Deborah Lee
b. 12-2-1957

Children of Frank Melvin

Orlin
b. 1893
m. Jewel Juneau.

Henry D. [2]
b.10-15-1895
d.10-15-1959 [3]
m. Linda Miller

Russel
b. 1-1-1925

Richard
b. 3-14-1931

Clifford
b. 12-24-1928

Dorothy
b. 8-4-1927

[*] Continued on own page.
[1] Died in Needles, Calif. at the hands of angry man over signs he had painted for him. Body never found by us.
[2] Concerning the family of Henry D. and Linda – Russel has no children. Dorothy – 1 daughter, Barbara, b. 1964; Clifford – son Bob, in army at Ft. Lee, VA.; Richard – 1 daughter, Karen – college at Ann Arbor, Mich, 1971.
[3] Died on his 64th birthday.
[4] Billy was later adopted by Edna. Edna married Frank after the death of Eva, who died young (age 22).

VALENTINE GENEALOGY

Harriet Flora Bennett
b. 3-14-1860
c. 6-10-1940

m. Rev. John D. Bennett

Baby Son
[died in infancy in Africa]

Fred
b. 1-31-1882
d. 1959
m. Della Montgomery

Baby Ruth
b. 1894
[died in infancy]

Paul
b. 1887
d. 1951
m. Mary Alice Wilcox

J.D.
b. 1900
m. Ethel Rhome
m. Gladys ?

Aurora Margaret *
b. 1-31-1904
m. Carl C. Weaver

Ellsworth
b. 1912
d. 1930 [age 18]

Roberta Justina
b. 2-29-1908
m. Michael Ruggieri

Ruth
b. 8-20-1916
m. George McFarlane

Dorothy
b. 1918
m. Henry Ostrander

Cynthia
b. 11-24-1946
Teacher

David
b. 3-14-1955

Robert Arthur
b. 11-10-1914
m. Florence
1 dau. Catherina
1 son. Robert
b. 9-28-1939
m. Helen

Paul Jr.
b. 5-31-1924
d. 8-15-1944

Marilyn
b. 1917
d. 1921

Carol Ann
b. 10-5-1937
m. Rummins

John
b. 8-21-1958

Nancy
b. 2-28-1963

Armand Bennett
b. 6-2-1930
m. Dorothy Wenbrecht

Linda
b. 5-7-1955
Deborah
b. 5-30-1954
Michael
b. 2-1-1957
Keith
b. 4-14-1962
Mark
b. 3-1-1967

Rolland Gene
b. 4-16-1934
m. Marta Garcia

Desiré
b. 7-23-1956
Michael
b. 6-23-1958
Albert
b. 2-11-1961
Joseph
b. 8-10-1969

Perry
b. 1943
m. Nancy Miller

Roderick
b. 1948

Jeff
b. 1-29-1967

Steven
b. 9-14-1968

Jennifer
b. 8-12-1969

Sally
b. 1950
m. James Cwiokala

Jimmie
b. 3-27-1970

Cheryl
b. 1952
m. Joseph Kowolski

John
b. 8-25-1971

Patricia Gail
b. 12-21-1936
m. Powers

Donald
b. 11-11-1955

Stephena
b. 4-6-1959

David
b. 12-14-1960

Cynthia
b. 5-7-1963

Roberta Joyce
b. 6-30-1940
m. Reinfrank

René
b. 1-31-1963

Daniel
b. 9-28-1967

* Continues on own page

SAGE/VALENTINE GENEALOGY

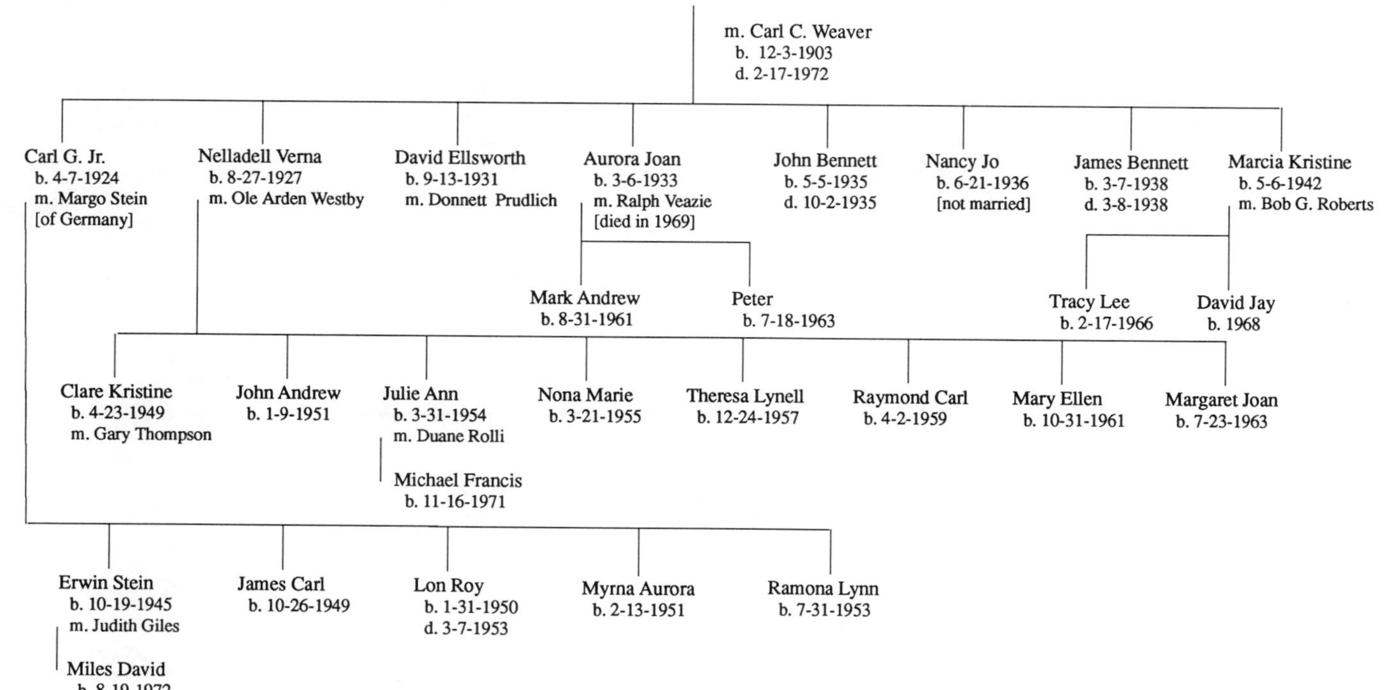

SAGE/VALENTINE GENEALOGY

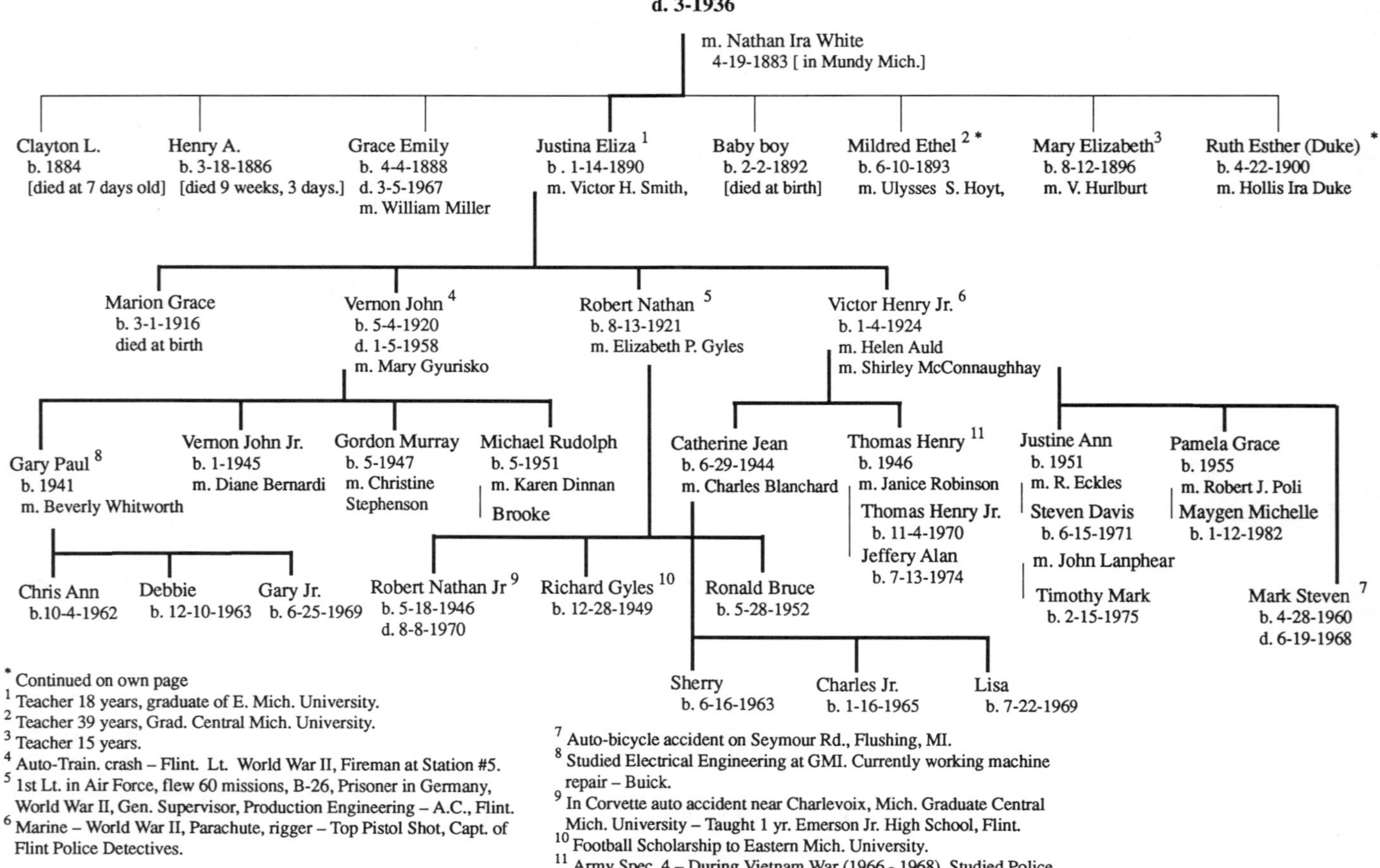

* Continued on own page
1 Teacher 18 years, graduate of E. Mich. University.
2 Teacher 39 years, Grad. Central Mich. University.
3 Teacher 15 years.
4 Auto-Train. crash – Flint. Lt. World War II, Fireman at Station #5.
5 1st Lt. in Air Force, flew 60 missions, B-26, Prisoner in Germany, World War II, Gen. Supervisor, Production Engineering – A.C., Flint.
6 Marine – World War II, Parachute, rigger – Top Pistol Shot, Capt. of Flint Police Detectives.
7 Auto-bicycle accident on Seymour Rd., Flushing, MI.
8 Studied Electrical Engineering at GMI. Currently working machine repair – Buick.
9 In Corvette auto accident near Charlevoix, Mich. Graduate Central Mich. University – Taught 1 yr. Emerson Jr. High School, Flint.
10 Football Scholarship to Eastern Mich. University.
11 Army Spec. 4 – During Vietnam War (1966 - 1968). Studied Police Administration, Flint Jr. College – Detective Flint Police.

WHITE GENEALOGY

George White
b. 1790
d. ?
m. Hannah Bronson [†]

Children of George White and Hannah Bronson:

- **Orson** — m. M. Pierce
  - Gard
  - Lucy (Wolcott)
    - Hannah [†]
- **George** — m. Julia Bachus
  - Charles
    - Louisa
  - Helen
    - Plianis
  - Mackie
  - Malinda
  - Laura (Baldwin)
    - Guy
- **Louisa** — b. 3-16-1818, d. 5-14-1853, m. Constance Beebe
  - E.
  - Mary Louisa [2] — Grandmother of Karen & Catherine Sherff, m. Raber
    - Winnifred — m. F. Sherff
- **Alpheus** [†] — b. 7-19-1819, d. 5-1893, m. Samantha Root [†1]
  - **Nathan Ira** [*] — b. 10-15-1858, d. 8-1-1945
  - **Mary** [*] — b. 1861, d. 1933
  - **Huldah** [*] — b. 11-11-1863, d. 4-13-1948
  - **James D.** — b. 10-17-1868, m. Winnifred Marshall
    - Abigail [Died in infancy]

  Children of Alpheus White line (next generation):
  - **Ermina** — m. Jerome White [3]
    - Elmer (Ida)
      - Myrtle
      - Alma
    - Wilkie (Bertha)
      - Orma Zelma Maude
  - **Lemuel** — m. Sadie Main
    - Baby Girl [died in infancy]
  - **John Nelson** — b. 1855, d. 1892, m. May Wilder
    - Maude (Byrle) — b. 10-8-1882, d. 4-13-1968, m. Ralph Arthur Carothers
      - William [died in infancy]
      - Marjorie — m. R. Pakes
        - Carolyn (Hanson)
        - Bobby
      - Glen — b. 1906, d. 1977
      - Mary Alice — b. 1907
      - Geraldine [died in infancy]
    - Baby Girl [died at birth]
- **Lemuel**
- **Isaac** [†] — b. 2-17-1830, d. 2-22-1905, m. Elizabeth Sage
- **Darwin**
- **Jane**
- **Mary**

[†] Photo on file.
[*] Continued on own page.
[1.] See Root Genealogy.
[2.] Died at birth of their baby son -- Eugene.
[3.] Real name was Adams; he was adopted.

WHITE GENEALOGY

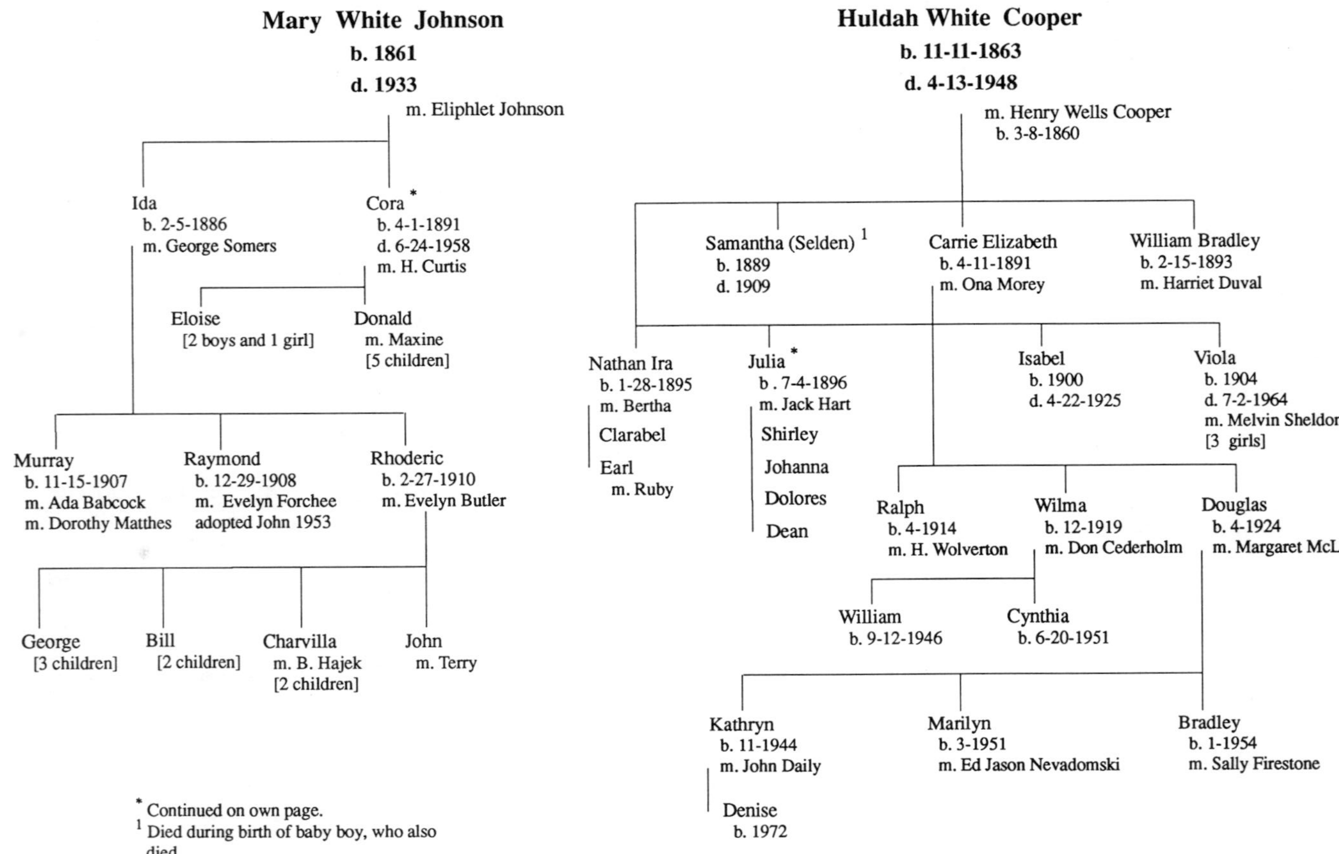

WHITE GENEALOGY

Nathan Ira White
b. 10-15-1858
d. 8-1-1945

married Esther Ann Sage

- Clayton
  1884
  [died at 7 days]

- Henry D.
  b. 3-18-1886
  [died 9 weeks, 3 days.]

- Grace Emily (Miller)
  b. 4-4-1888
  d. 3-5-1967

- Justina Eliza (Smith) [1]
  b . 1-14-1890
  m. Victor H. Smith

- Baby boy
  b. 2-2-1892
  [died at birth]

- Mildred Ethel [2] *
  b. 6-10-1893
  m. Ulysses S. Hoyt

- Mary Elizabeth [3]
  (Hurlburt)
  b. 8-12-1896

- Ruth Esther (Duke) *
  b. 4-22-1900
  m. Hollis Ira Duke

Children of Justina Eliza (Smith):

- Marion Grace
  b. 3-1-1916
  [died at birth]

- Vernon John * [4]
  b. 5-4-1920
  d. 1-5-1958
  m. Mary Gyurisko [divorced]
  m. Velta Beavers

- Robert Nathan * [5]
  8-13-1921
  m. Elizabeth P. Gyles

- Victor Henry Jr. [6]
  b. 1-4-1924
  m. Helen Auld [divorced]
  m. Shirley McConnaughhay

Children:

- Catherine Jean
  b. 6-29-1944
  m. Charles Blanchard [divorced]
  m. John Hearsch

  - Sherry Lynn
    b. 6-16-1963
    m. Steven Jackson
    - Ashley Nicole
      b. 1-7-1987
  - Charles L. Blanchard
    b. 1-16-1965
  - Lisa Ellen
    b. 7-22-1969

- Thomas Henry Sr. [9]
  b. 11-9-1946
  m. Janice Robinson [divorced]
  m. Sue A. Burtch
  - Thomas Henry Jr.
    b. 11-4-1970
  - Jeffrey A.
    b. 7-13-1974
  - Amy Kathryn [adopted]
    b. 11-24-1987

- Justine Ann
  b. 12-1-1951
  m. Rick Eckels [divorced]
  m. John Lanphear
  - Stephen D. [8]
    b. 6-15-1971
  - Timothy M.
    b. 2-15-1975

- Pamela Grace
  b. 1-22-1955
  m. Robert J. Poli
  - Maygen M.
    b. 1-12-1982

- Mark Steven [7]
  b. 4-28-1960
  d. 6-19-1968

* Continued on own page.
[1] Taught school for 18 years
[2] Taught shcool for 39 years.
[3] Taught school for 15 years.
[4] Auto-train accident. Lt. in Air Force, World War II.
[5] 1st Lt. in Air Force, flew 60 missions, Prisoner of War, World War II, General Supervisor Production, Engineering at A.C.
[6] Marine in World War II, Top Pistol Shot, Capt. of Flint Detectives.
[7] Auto-bike accidental death.
[8] Stephen was adopted by John Lanphear.
[9] Served in U.S. Army during Vietnam War. Detective Sgt. Flint Police Dept.

WHITE GENEALOGY

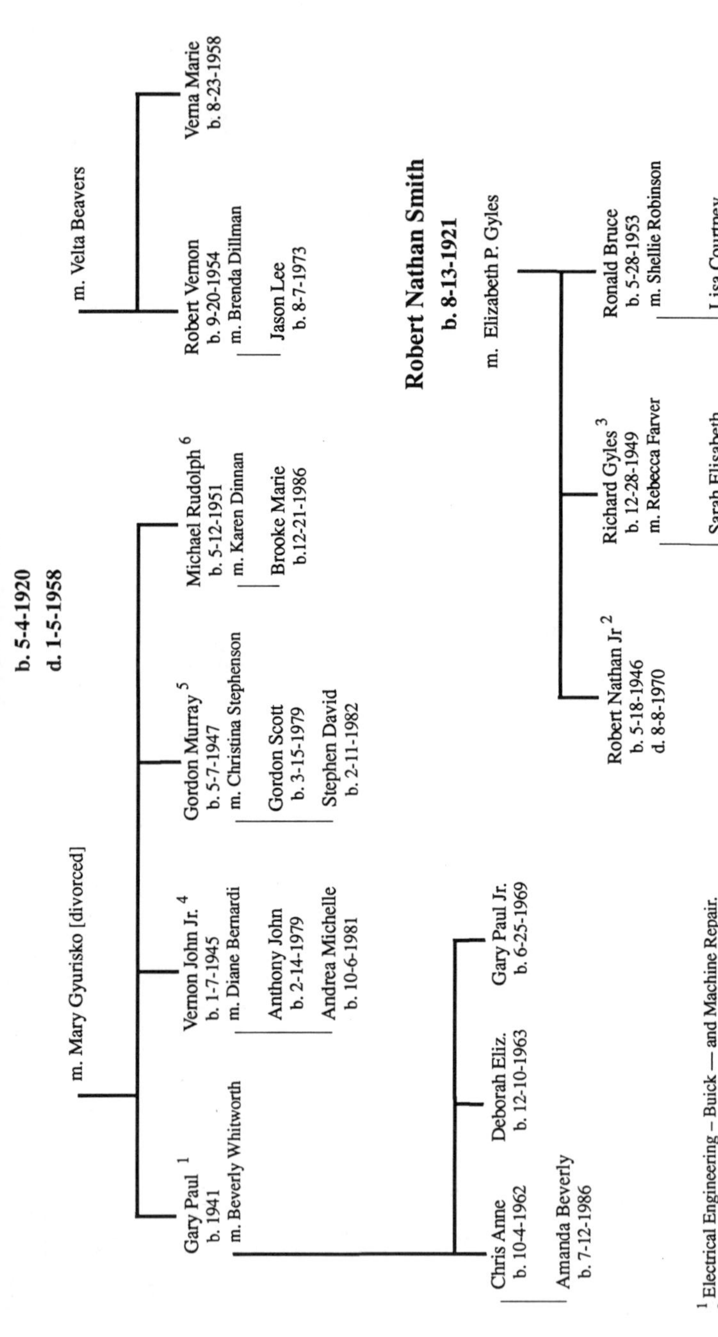

1 Electrical Engineering – Buick — and Machine Repair.
2 Corvette auto accident – age 24. Grad of C.S. Teachers College, taught one year.
3 College Football Scholarship.
4 Graduate U. of Mich. (Flint) – District Superintendent, Consumers Power Co.
5 Graduate Eastern Mich. University – Dir. Vocational Ed., Genesee Co., Intermediate School District.
6 Studying U. of Mich. (Flint), Supervisor, Energy Services, Consumers Power Co.

WHITE GENEALOGY

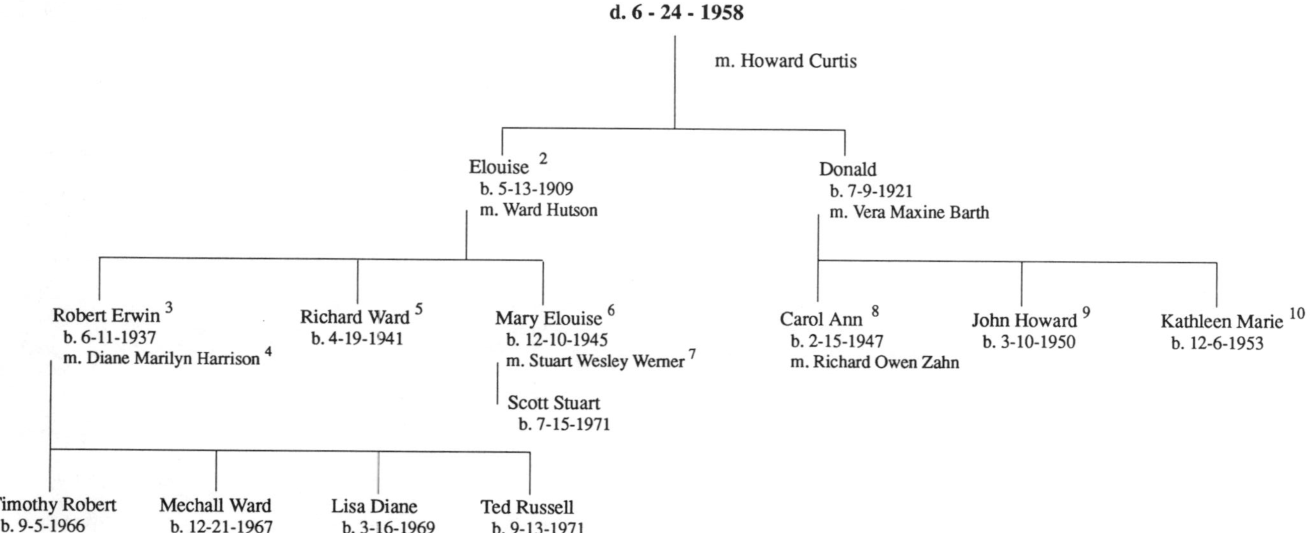

Cora Johnson Curtis [1]
b. 4 - 1 - 1891
d. 6 - 24 - 1958

m. Howard Curtis

Elouise [2]
b. 5-13-1909
m. Ward Hutson

Donald
b. 7-9-1921
m. Vera Maxine Barth

Robert Erwin [3]
b. 6-11-1937
m. Diane Marilyn Harrison [4]

Richard Ward [5]
b. 4-19-1941

Mary Elouise [6]
b. 12-10-1945
m. Stuart Wesley Werner [7]

Scott Stuart
b. 7-15-1971

Carol Ann [8]
b. 2-15-1947
m. Richard Owen Zahn

John Howard [9]
b. 3-10-1950

Kathleen Marie [10]
b. 12-6-1953

Timothy Robert
b. 9-5-1966

Mechall Ward
b. 12-21-1967

Lisa Diane
b. 3-16-1969

Ted Russell
b. 9-13-1971

[1] D aughter of Mary White Johnson and Great Grandaughter of George White.
[2] Grad. of Linden H.S. 1927
[3] Grad of Alma College – B. A. 1959.
[4] Grad St. Philip H. S. and Business College
[5] Grad. – Stockbridge H. S. '54. Grad Northwestern. B.A. – 1963. M.A. 1964. H.B.D·
[6] Grad. Stockbridge H.S. '64. Alma College – 1968.
[7] Grad – Allegan H.S. 1957. W.M.U. – 3 yrs.
[8] Grad – Stockbridge H.S. '65. Cleary College. Med. Sec. to Orthopedic Surgeon in Ann Arbor
[9] Grad – S.H.S. Jackson Col. 2 yrs. – also Ferris Col. 1 term. Drives milk route in Stockbridge
[10] Grad – S.H.S., Ferris College – '73. Studying to be commercial artist.

WHITE GENEALOGY

Julia Cooper Hart [1]
b. 7-4-1896

m. Jack Hart

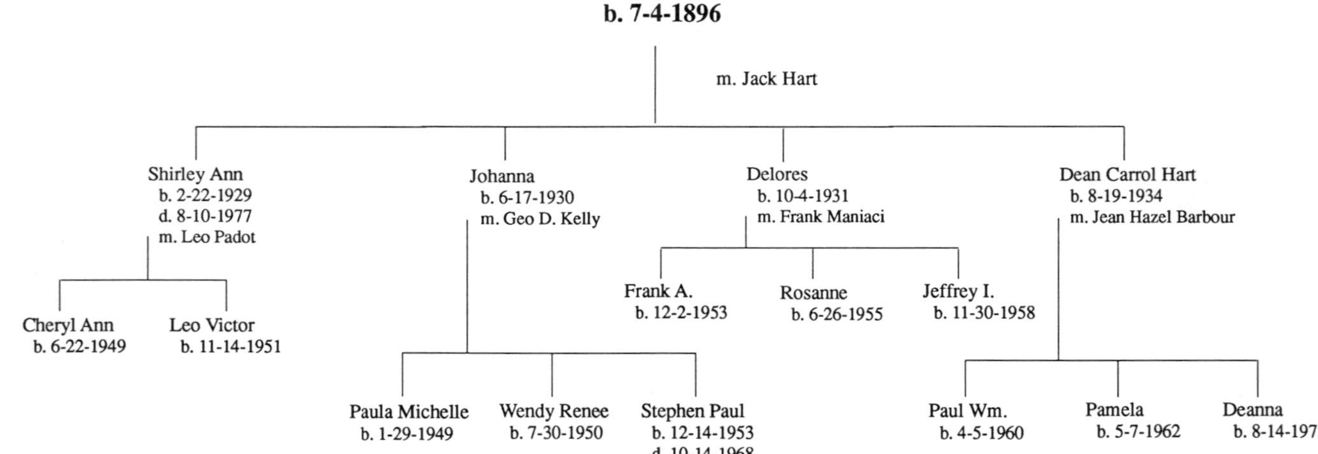

[1] Daughter of Hulda White Cooper and
Great Grandaughter of George White

ROOT GENEALOGY
Grandma Samantha Root – White-Steven's Family

William Root

m. Mary

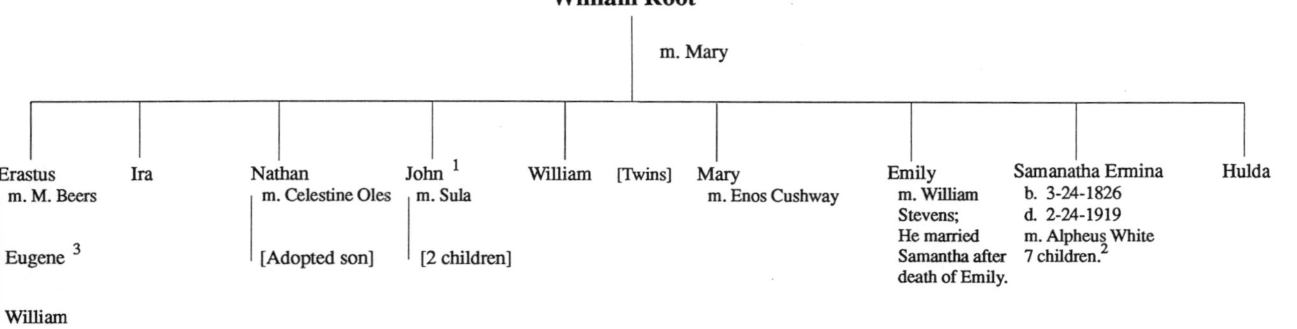

[1] He was a fife player.
[2] See White Genealogy and marriage to William Stevens (her brother-in-law) after death of Alpheus White. She died in 1919 at age 93. Came to Michigan with parents from birth place (Auburn, NY) at age 7. Settled near Plymouth.
[3] Ruth & Margaret Beers – Descendants.

CHAPTER II

PODUNK AND THE DAKOTA TERRITORY

TO REALLY UNDERSTAND my writing I believe it's important to read about the adventurous early settlers who provided the backdrop for my extended performance here.

Before Michigan was accepted into the Union of States it was traversed by many different peoples. The natives found here by European explorers are now thought of as being of Oriental extraction. They, in general, populated this great new space very sparsely. I do know what they should have been called rightfully, but the name Indian, given to them, was incorrect.

I like what the Australians called their natives, Aborigines. These people of North America should have been named Americans. But as long as the word Indian has been accepted for general use I shall have to conform to this precedent. So here we go.

Indian trails, which were really only paths where people could walk single file, followed the ridges and high ground. For local Indians these trails connected waterways such as the Shiawassee and Flint Rivers. Trading posts were first established at the convergence of trails and rivers by fur trading companies.

Next came the white settlers who built waterpowered mills which in most instances became villages. Out of necessity the

Indian trails were improved and became roads. They were named after the villages. Linden Road is an excellent example. Some of the other local roads were Baldwin, Grand Blanc, Saginaw, Fenton and Miller. I have been told that the Miller Road which meandered south and west from the Grand Traverse of the Flint River was first known as the Otterburn Trail.

As the Indians succumbed to the diseases and vices of the white man, which decimated their already thin population, many of the natural resources were taken over by people like my forefathers. Some of these were the waterways, trails, sugar maple forests, wild game, fish, wild berries etc. The area has been labeled by others as the "Palm of the Mitten."

Podunk in Genesee County which was located a bit east from Torrey road and south of Baldwin Road proved to be an area to their liking. Although as far as I have been able to find out none of the members of our four families that are listed in the genealogy chart ever lived in the pioneer trading post of De-Mon-E-Wink (Podunk.) They could have been members of the crew that worked for George Judson digging the ditch from Pleasant Lake (Lake Fenton) which was a distance of nearly two miles to feed the millpond at Podunk and thus provide power for the mills. One was a sawmill. Another was a linseed oil mill which pressed flaxseeds so firmly that they yielded valuable oil, leaving a material called linseed meal which was great livestock feed. This mill was operated by the LaTourette family, ancestors of the late Sheldon LaTourette who was a great influence on the agricultural population of the county. Finally, there was the gristmill which was the essential. Other businesses were a blacksmith shop and White's General Store, an extension of the original trading post. A school was built on the corner of Baldwin and Torrey Roads called the O'Dell which was about two hundred rods north of the dozen or so houses in Podunk. Another early school was located at the northeast corner of Linden and Baldwin Roads called the White. Podunk became, quite naturally, a place of gathering where nice dances were held and other social events such as swimming in the summer and skating during the winter at the millpond. The White's were a musical family and two of the boys became good fiddle players. They were much in demand to play at schoolhouse dances, winter house parties and summer barn raisings. The Sage and White families became acquainted at social events held at Podunk.

Sometime around 1845 a United States Postoffice was built on the grounds of what is now the Lake Fenton High School when developers plotted land and named the place Mt. Pleasant. Their plans for a town did not materialize as expected and during 1851 this postoffice was transferred to George Judson's place in Podunk where most of the people lived. Mail was picked up in Flint three days a week. Reuben Sage is listed as being one of the postmasters of Mundy Postoffice.

The Genesee County Atlas of 1873 listed at least twelve parcels of Mundy Township land as being owned by families of my lineage. Not all of my people were landowners. I am certain others lived on rented land, were laborers or owned land in adjoining Genesee County Townships which I did not get to look into before my eyesight deteriorated to its present condition.

My parents naturally met at Podunk. My mother, Esther Ann Sage, got her eye on John White but it was too late or too little because he got out of her sight temporarily and went off and married up with someone else. After a healing period my mother became interested in John's brother, Nathan White. He was the other fiddle player. They were married April 19, 1883 at the residence of Henry D. Sage, Mundy, Michigan by a circuit riding Free Methodist minister, Reverend F. A. Godwin, who preached when available at the local Free Methodist Church on Thompson Road. The building still stands and is used as a residence.

All the young people in the vicinity of Thompson Road, including those of my family, attended this Free Methodist Church and all went forward and were converted. The White boys, after being converted, felt they had a higher calling for their life's work than playing for dances, so they stopped rosining up their bows, put the violins in their cases and stepped off the dance floors never to return.

My Uncle John White took up his calling to be a minister right away and made it his life's work, but my father, Nathan White, had to help his father with the family farm that my grandpa had mortgaged heavily. The farm was right next to the corner of Baldwin and Sharp Roads. My great-aunt, Laura Baldwin, had found the spot first and built a beautiful house

PANORAMIC VIEW OF SAGE STEADING

L to R: Uncle Clayton Sage, Grandpa Henry, Grandma Ann, Aunt Nettie, Aunt Ida and Uncle William Sage. This photo bears in-depth viewing.

MY MOTHER

*Esther Ann Sage was photographed in
1875 at the age of eighteen.*

there, which stands today. My grandfather, Alpheus White,
(Laura's brother) chose the 40 acres next to hers and built a small
but nice house there. They both built their homes about the time
of their marriages and about the time Michigan became a state.

My father was born in 1858, one of seven children. He
helped his father farm the land and it was there he took his bride,
Esther Ann Sage, to live when they were married. They were not
able to afford a place of their own.

In 1884 a beautiful baby boy was born to my mother and
father, but there was something wrong with him and they didn't
know then what it was. The baby died after three months of
agony. He was buried beside his great-grandmother.

In 1885 another little boy was born with the same problem and also died. My father felt so bad and blamed himself. He decided to go out west by himself to the Dakota Territory; this was before it became a state. He found some land near Seneca, Dakota, located later in South Dakota, bought a horse and plow and decided to farm. He built a little house by himself in the side of a hill, covered it with sod similar to other houses that had been built on the plains at that time. He put out a vegetable and flower garden before sending for my mother in 1886. My mother loved that little sod house! She often talked about it in detail to anyone who would listen.

In the winter of 1886 they weathered a very bad blizzard. So severe that they strung a rope from the house to the barn so they could find their way out to feed the horse.

In 1887 Grandpa Sage went out to the Territory to see how they were getting along. He helped them all spring with their crops. As he was preparing to leave and go back home to Michigan, he looked out and saw a yellow haze and realized it was a prairie fire. He had Nathan get out his plow and plow all around the house and barn. When the prairie fire roared past, it came right up to the plowed line. They had to keep the house and barn wet and even mother had to put a wet sheet over her hair to keep it from burning.

After the fire, grandpa thought they should go back to Michigan because of all the hardships. But my father wanted to·stay. My mother said nothing though she was thinking a lot. So my grandpa went back to Michigan alone.

Then, lo and behold! my mother found she was pregnant again. That winter of 1887, when my mother was pregnant, they survived another bad blizzard. When the baby was born on April 4, 1888, it was a joyous occasion. It was a beautiful baby girl — perfect in every way. They named her Grace Emily. When the Sage grandparents heard about the baby, Grandpa Sage again came out to the Dakota Territory that summer to see the baby and see how they were faring.

Then in the winter of 1888 the worst blizzard ever recorded hit the Dakota Territory. My parents could only stay inside their little sod house until the storm subsided. The morning after the storm died down they sat down and talked it over. Again dad wanted to stay but this time mother said, "No, I can't." She felt if she were to have another baby there, they would never make it.

My parents had unshakable faith and after thinking it through and putting their faith in God, they made the right decision to come back to Michigan.

There was a lot of work to be done before leaving Dakota that fall of 1889. They sold their horse and plow, and after salvaging as much of their crops as they could they packed what articles they could take with them and headed for home. They arrived home after a trying journey to a joyful meeting with their parents. Grandpa White was especially glad they were back as he had not been well and needed help on the farm. Their other children were married and gone. My mother, being pregnant again, was also glad to be home. After settling down in dear old Michigan they were ready to meet any emergency — they were home!

I have always retained an intense positive feeling about this land of Michigan. Could this viewpoint have been acquired by inheritance?

CHAPTER III

A FAIR-HAIRED BABY GIRL

ON JANUARY 14, 1890 a beautiful fair-haired baby girl entered upon the scene. I was named Justina for my Grandma Sage and Eliza for my great-aunt, my Grandpa Sage's sister. This is where my life story really begins.

The title I have chosen for my autobiography is "Tina", my nickname, with emphasis on the state of Michigan which has always been a part of me and which I love.

And it is indeed a Wonderland! As children, when we look at the stars we wonder what they are "up above the world so high like diamonds in the sky." When we get older we know that they are distant suns shining by their own light, probably with planets revolving around them. What a wonderful world God has made! Because the earth moves and tilts toward and then away from the sun, it causes the four seasons. These four seasons are at their best in Michigan because we are in the north temperate zone. The lower peninsula of Michigan, on a map, looks like a mitten that was dropped down in the middle of beautiful fresh water and pushed five lakes to their boundaries. It has the longest shoreline of any state.

Using as basis, an act passed in 1945 by the Michigan Legislature declaring that the area of the state to be 96,720 square miles it is the largest state east of the Mississippi River.

Michigan's economy is supported by three basic industries, manufacturing, agriculture and tourism. As far as I could find out they are about equal. The automobile is the reason Michigan has done so well in manufacturing. At one time most of them were made here. Agriculture and natural resources have been important since the land was first settled and remains so. Michigan leads all states in the production of cherries and navy beans. Livestock and their products account for one-half of all farm income. As far as tourism goes I think Michigan has more boats and sells more hunting and fishing licenses than any other state. By reading on you will note that in the company of my immediate family I have traveled this beautiful state, that God has given us to enjoy, and I believe that as time goes on Michigan will be regarded more highly as a place for vacationing than it has been during my lifetime — if the environment we now have is protected and maintained.

I was conceived in the Dakota Territory at about the time it ceased to be. I never went back. During 1889 this territory was twained into North and South Dakota and both were admitted into the great union that makes up this nation as the 39th and 40th states. There has been a mystery or unexplained force in my life for all of these years which I have never fully understood or perhaps never should. This is only a conjecture. Was there a fear, brooded over and harbored by my mother, instilled into me before birth about the Dakota Territory because of the three killer blizzards and the terrifying prairie fire? Also, as a direct reaction is this why I never cared for the treeless wide open spaces and never journeyed to the Dakotas although I had plenty of opportunities? In reverse, could this be why I have always been so in love with Michigan?

CHAPTER IV

EARLY DAYS ON THE FARM

MY FIRST REMEMBRANCE was when I was about three years old. Not only were we living with Grandpa and Grandma White, but my cousin, Maude (Uncle John's daughter) was also living with them. Her mother and father had died leaving her an orphan at nine.

What fun we had on the farm! I used to love to help grandma pick peas and beans and gather eggs and help her churn. After churning she would place the butter in a wooden bowl and shape it with a ladle. Then she would put it in crocks and take it to the store to exchange for groceries. It was a great experience going to town and looking at everything in the stores. I would dream about it later.

My grandmother was an immaculate housekeeper and such a good cook. She would let me help her make pies with the apples from the orchard and from elderberries gathered along the rail fence. There were many different apple trees in the orchard. Northern Spy, Snow, Talman Sweet, Greening, Greasy Pippin and Russet were some of them. In the fall grandma would can apples for use during the winter. She would also dry some by putting pieces on stringers in the kitchen. It would attract so many flies I would hold the door open while the grown people chased them out with dish towels.

Grandma would also let me help her in the flower garden. There were forget-me-nots, nasturtiums, batchelor buttons, sunflowers and many, many more. Grandma's flower garden was so beautiful that people passing by would stop their horses just to admire it.

While living with grandma and grandpa they taught me many things I could use in later life. It was part of my education. They were such marvelous people!

I loved the outdoors and would help my Pa get the horse and plow and walk behind him in the fields. As the corn came up we would put scarecrows in the fields to keep the birds from pulling the corn. Also, I would help grandpa in his orchard. How beautiful it was when the trees were in bloom, with the bees buzzing about. Grandma told me if you didn't bother the bees they wouldn't sting you, and she was right! They would land on my face and never sting.

One day one of the mares got into the green apples on the ground under the trees. She ate so many apples that she died, even though Pa gave her some medicine to try to help. After the horse (Jenny was her name) died, Pa replaced her with a Hamiltonian which we named Maggie. She was a mean and unpredictable horse. The other horse was named Mike. Maggie would nip at him if she was upset. For instance, if the wagon wheels would hit a rut in the road and cause the tongue of the wagon to hit Maggie, she would bite Mike.

Another early remembrance is sitting on my grandpa's lap. He would have candies for me and would hide them on the window sill so my sister, Grace, couldn't get them.

Every morning my father would take down the family Bible and we would kneel at our chairs and have family prayer. My mother and father taught me the Bible before I was able to read. After I was old enough to go to church I loved to read the Bible myself.

When I was three and Grace was five we both had scarlet fever. The doctor came with his little black bag and poured out some powder for us to take. We were quarantined. After about six weeks we were feeling better. Then we had to fumigate the house

"UNALIKE" SISTERS

Justina and Grace White at two and four years. Photo taken in 1892 in a walnut corner chair while all dressed up in buttoned shoes, matching mother-made winter dresses with cocheted collars. We were as different as night and day in temperament.

by burning sulphur. Grace had it harder than I did and it took her much longer to recover. Pa and Ma were good nurses so we returned to good health.

I loved books and my first school experience was just great. I still have my entrance card for school dated 1894. After I learned to read the teacher would let me read by standing in front of the class. I always said I wanted to be a teacher and when I was young I would play school with my dolls lined up as pupils.

My Aunt Huldah and her family lived about a half mile west of us on Baldwin Road. After school I would stop at her house and she would give me bread and butter with molasses on it. I would say, "Aunt Huddie, I want a piece of bread and butter with 'lasses on it." Aunt Huldah had two little girls, Samantha and Carrie. Samantha was about my age and we had great fun together. No matter how much noise we made Aunt Huldah would never reprimand us, but join in the fun. Grace and Cousin Maude were just the opposite of me. They had their "aristocratic" friends and didn't join in the fun as much as I did at Aunt Huldah's.

Grace was always so precise. At the table she would say, "Please pass the butter," but I would say, "Give me some butter." One day at the table I could hardly wait till my father finished the long blessing. So as soon as he finished, I yelled, "Hurrah, pitch in!" Well, Pa made me leave the table—but only for five minutes and then he let me come back. He tried to teach us good table manners. I can remember him helping us cut up our pancakes into little squares and telling us to eat one square at a time so the syrup didn't run down our chins. My mother was strict with us but she was not very well and always busy with the household chores so Pa was the one doing most of the disciplining. I remember when we weren't feeling well he would put some bad tasting medicine in a spoon, but put sugar on top to make it taste better before giving it to us. He called the medicine "steketee" whatever that meant. Medicine was almost non-existent in those days. It could have been some Indian remedy.

Because Pa could make anything grow everyone said he had a green thumb. I always looked for his green thumb but never happened to see it.

My grandpa died when I was three years and five months old. I was coming home from Aunt Huldah's when I saw flowers

In Kind Remembrance

OF THE

FALL TERM OF 1894.

BEEBE DISTRICT, GAINES, MICH.

MINNIE COON, TEACHER.

Names of Pupils.

FLORA SMITH,
CLIFTON SMITH,
MILLIARD SMITH,
FLOYD SMITH,
DILLIE PROPPER,
BEN PROPPER,
WELTHA PROPPER,
DORA PROPPER,
ADA MUNDY,
VENINA VINCENT,
ELMER SHAW,
FRANK PEARSAL,
NETELA ORMINSON,
VEVA BEERS, (Snow)
VENA BURNHAM,
EVA BURNHAM,
BEN BLAIR,
EDDIE BREWER,

FLOYD BREWER,
LEONARD McCOMB,
MARTIN JEWELL,
HENRY EISENTRIGER,
JAMES PROPPER,
MABEL BREWER,
CALVIN BENEDICT,
GRACIE WHITE,
MAUD WHITE,
LAURA BORTON,
AVA ORMINSON,
ELSIE EISENTRIGER,
IDA JOHNSON,
ELVIN DOWNER,
FRED DOWNER,
TINA WHITE, (age 4)
BLANCHE BREWER.
(Benedict)

TREASURED REMEMBRANCES

BEEBE, MY FIRST SCHOOL

Located on the northwest corner of Beers and Baldwin Roads, it was built in 1877 and destroyed by fire while being used as a residence in 1980. It was called, legally, Fractional District No. 1 Gaines and Mundy. It was the last one room country school in Genesee to close. This photo was taken in June 1966 with Tina (White) Smith standing in the doorway where she began her education at age 4.

and ribbons on the door. When I went in grandpa was lying in a big box. Pa lifted me up to look and I asked if grandpa was sleeping. I wanted him to wake up but he didn't move — I thought that was odd. I hung on to the casket so long I pulled the braid off and Pa had to have a man come out to tack it back on.

Not long after this episode I was coming home from Aunt Huldah's again a little bit earlier than they expected me. Pa met me and I didn't see Ma anywhere. He showed me a big white bundle in a chair. I thought it was the puppy I had been wanting, when I saw the bundle move. But when I opened it, it was a little baby — my new sister, Mildred. Pa asked me if I wouldn't rather play with a baby than a dog. Of course, I said yes. And we did have fun playing out-of-doors with the baby that summer. I was always closer to Mildred than my other sisters.

We had such great fun when Uncle Ike would come to visit. (He was Grandpa White's brother.) He was short and stocky with black hair and a black beard down to his waist. He would toss the baby, Mildred, up in the air when we would play and shout and sing nursery rhymes. Then he would bring old Mike up to the fence and put Mildred and me on him and walk us around the field. I remember once he said, "See that bull in the field? I can ride him, too." He went over, jumped on him and rode him around the field. Uncle Ike was a "corker" and so happy-go-lucky, we loved to have him visit.

One bright sunny day in the late summer of 1894 I was sitting under the sweet apple tree that grandpa had planted by the front gate. (He planted it there especially so people going by could stop and have an apple.) A beautiful buggy with a man and woman drove up and stopped. I ran into the house to tell grandma someone was coming. He got out and helped the lady out. What a handsome couple. He was dressed finer than I had ever seen anyone dressed and sporting a big handlebar mustache. His wife was dressed in a fine silk dress and a shawl with fringe. She wore beautiful high heeled shoes with pointed toes and buttons. On her head was the most beautiful bonnet ever, with her curls showing all around. She didn't say a word but my grandmother met them at the door and seemed to know them and what they wanted. I heard the words "mortgage" and "foreclosure", words I had heard before. Then Pa came in from the fields to talk with them. I found out they were the banker and his wife from Flint. He said it had been a year since a payment had been made on the farm and they had to foreclose. My grandmother cried and begged them to wait one more year as they were doing better and were likely to get some money together soon. But they were stern and said they had already waited a year. They got out the papers and said, "Sign here." So my grandmother and Ma and Pa had to sign the foreclosure papers. I thought if I had to sign I would not do it. But, of course, I didn't. After signing off the farm, the

CORKER OF THE CLAN

My Uncle, Isaac White and his wife Aunt Eliza (Sage), photographed on their 43rd wedding anniversary September 20, 1897, around the time people from the White and Sage families intermarried. They had no children. He was a humorous man.

banker said they would give us till the next spring to move. The farm was gone! There were a few more tears but, of course, you do what you have to do.

That fall we butchered the hogs, canned and dried fruit — we could have anything we could take with us. I watched the butchering and didn't like it one bit. After catching the hogs and killing them they would put them on big sticks and pass them back and forth in big kettles of hot water and ashes so they could scrape off the hair and clean the skin before taking out their guts. They cured the hams and put them in the smokehouse and cut the meat in sections. Grandma didn't waste any of the meat, not even the heads, but made headcheese. It was processed so none was wasted. Some she gave to the neighbors and some to Aunt Huldah. What hogs weren't butchered we sold at an auction sale. We also sold the cows and chickens. We could keep the money from anything we sold but the beautiful apple trees stayed with the farm. There was no way Pa could take them.

During that fall of 1894, while my parents were preparing to leave the farm, I started my first full year of school. My teacher was a man named Thomas Stiff. I was a little afraid of him because I thought he had a funny name. I soon got used to him and he helped me learn to read whole sentences from a chart.

That Christmas of 1894 was the first Christmas I remember and I remember it so well. We hung up our stockings and Christmas morning in my stocking was a beautiful doll with blond painted hair. Grace had a doll in her stocking, too, just like mine except hers had dark painted hair. Mine I named Daisy and she named hers Pearl. I still have my doll to this day! No one could touch her because I loved her so much.

CHAPTER V

DURAND, STANTON AND COLEMAN

URING THE WINTER of 1894–1895 Pa was looking for another place to live. He heard about a man near Durand who wanted someone to come and farm his place. In 1895 we moved to Durand to a beautiful big brick house. We lived in a part of it. I remember how pretty the windows looked with stained glass around all of them. We liked everything we saw when we got there. Grace and I started school that fall near Durand. However, we didn't like the school very well. I believe it was called the Mikan School.

One day we came home from visiting the neighbors and we didn't see Ma anywhere. A lady by the name of Almeda Peck met us at the door and told us to be quiet. She led us to the bedroom where Ma was lying and we heard a little baby crying. To our surprise there was another little sister. She was so cute and had little curls all over her head. Ma said, "This is Mary Elizabeth." How glad we were for another little sister to play with. She was born August 12, 1896.

When we moved to Durand grandma went to live with Aunt Huldah on Baldwin Road. While there she became reacquainted with her late sister's husband (her sister had passed away some years ago) and they were married. His name was Mr. William

SEPTEMBER MARRIAGE

My Grandfather Alpheus died when I was 3 in May, 1893. Grandma Saman-tha (Root) went to live with Aunt Huldah in Stanton where she married William Stevens who owned a hotel and opera house there. This had a great influence on our immediate family

Stevens and he had owned and operated the hotel and opera house in Stanton. He also owned a farm near Palo (south of Stanton) and needed someone to run it. Grandma thought that would be a good opportunity for Pa because he could someday buy it after working it for a few years. After much thought Pa decided to take advantage of this opportunity and we moved to Stanton.

We lived with grandma for awhile in the hotel and then moved to a house we rented for $3.00 a month. It was a nice house and Pa, with his green thumb, had a beautiful garden. We moved there in 1896 and I started third grade in Stanton that fall. Grace was in the fourth grade then. I remember my teacher's

STANTON, MICHIGAN 1884

The town as I remember it as a small child. Included is the Green School which I attended later.

name was Nora Markee, a very nice teacher. She would use her blackboard pointer to tap time on the floor so we could learn to march.

My teacher in the fifth grade at Stanton was my pride and joy, my favorite teacher of all time. Her name was Lucinda Gilpin. I adored that girl and she took right to me, too. She was so pretty with a beautiful complexion. She wore such pretty clothes and shoes and perfume every day. Her voice was so sweet I would ask her to help me just to hear her speak. Lucinda told my mother I could do sixth grade work. While in the fifth grade we had a spelldown and I could outspell everyone in the sixth grade. I remember the word that I finally misspelled was "foulard" which was a kind of cloth. It was such a funny word, I had never heard of it. How could I spell it?

In 1900 my little sister, Ruth, was born while we lived in Stanton. When she was born, my teacher, Lucinda Gilpin, came to see her and asked what we had named her. My family wanted

OUR TRANSPORTATION

Going and coming by train for young girls was safe, dependable, inexpensive and fun. I liked to sit in the window and watch fancy dressed people get off the train and have "Colonel" Vaughn with his fancy rig and high stepping horses take them to the Stevens Hotel.

to name her Nellie but Lucinda said she had a horse named Nellie and suggested the name "Ruth", so that's what we named her.

While Ruth was just a baby she got the whooping cough. One day she was choking severely when Pa came home. He quickly took her outside and threw her up in the air. This helped her catch her breath and saved her life, mother said.

In Stanton, our house was near the depot and a few blocks from the hotel. We used to love to watch "Colonel" Vaughn, who owned a double surrey. He met passengers from the trains and took them and their baggage to the hotel. He had two Dalmation dogs who would stay right under the surrey and when "Colonel" Vaughn would start up with his high stepping team of driving horses they would trot behind. They were beautiful well behaved dogs.

Another favorite thing to do was play in the yard on a teeter-totter and swing Pa had made from a stump and a long board. He put a hinge on it so we could swing around on the stump or teeter totter. What fun we had living there! All the kids in town came to our place to play on the contraption Pa made for us.

While in the fifth grade at Stanton I met a girl who pulled a mean trick on me. She knew that a boy by the name of Victor Smith liked me very much so she made up a note, signed my name to it and gave it to him. The note said that he could take me home from the prayer meeting at the Baptist Church the next evening. When I came out of church he stepped up to me and took my arm and wanted to take me home. I knew he was younger than I was, so I told him, "No, you can't take me home, you are too young and too little!" When he told me about the note, I told him I did not write it and ran away from him. All the children teased me about that for a long time. It was hard to live down.

One day Pa received a letter from Leonard Sage, a distant cousin of ma's, who owned a sawmill near Coleman, Michigan. He offered such good wages Pa realized it was a better situation for all of us. We packed up and moved to Coleman. Before we moved Pa went ahead to Coleman and built a little tar paper shanty near the sawmill for us to live in. There were shanties built for all the workers at this large sawmill. The cook's shanty was Shanty #1, Leonard's brother, Charles, lived in Shanty #2 and ours was Shanty #3. We all loved this little shanty, because it was the first home that was really ours. It had one large room and two small rooms that were the bedrooms. Pa had a little job on his own cutting cedar fence posts and I would help him by pulling the cross-cut saw. Since he didn't have any sons I loved to help him.

The school at Coleman was about two miles from where we lived but if we cut through the woods or walked down the railroad track it was only about one mile. Only one train a day used the track and we would wait for the train each day. The engineer, with a red bandana around his neck, would wave to us. Sometimes we would put two pins crosswise on the tracks and when the train would run over them they would form a little pair of scissors.

We lived right on the edge of a deep woods and my younger sister, Mildred, and I would spend a lot of time climbing trees,

MY SUNDAY SCHOOL CLASS IN STANTON

Girls in Free Methodist Sunday School Class, 1898.
L to R, top row; Pearl McDrew, Mertie Zenholf, Lillian Cunningham.
Middle Row; Leta Gootnary, my sister Grace White, our teacher Sister
Perkins. I am sitting on the floor in the foreground.

swinging from the branches of the hemlocks and listening to the various birds. I spent so much time listening that I could imitate all the bird calls.

Our horses, Mike and Maggie, were still with us when we lived in Coleman and Maggie was still mean. I teased her a lot by tickling her on the nose with a straw while she was eating her hay. She didn't like that and would lunge at me. One day Pa asked me to get the horses from the pasture. I had to go down the road we called the "Green Tunnel Road." It was called that because the tall grass and the tree leaves nearly came together. As I stopped to pick some wildflowers to take home I heard a horse running behind me. I turned to see Maggie chasing me with her teeth bared. I ran as fast as I could and found a place under the barbed wire fence where I could just squeeze through. Luckily that hole

BUNKHOUSE AT SAGE'S SAWMILL

With six lumberjacks, two cooks including Maggie Sage on the far right, and two Sage children, Pearl and George. Notice several small trees protruding through tar paper roof.

SAGE'S LUMBER CAMP NEAR COLEMAN, MICHIGAN, 1900

Log pile, people and horses and the Sage Sawmill near Coleman where we lived and Dad worked. L to R; George Sage, Maggie Sage, Mary White, Me at age 11, Mother holding Ruth, Mildred, Pearl Sage, Camp Cook Mrs. Smith, George Searsaw. On the ground L to R; Charles Sage, Leonard Sage Jr. holding first team, My Dad, holding second, Uncle Leonard Sage, owner, Mr. Smith with last team. What a team!

was there or Maggie would have killed me. Finally I got her calmed down and she followed Mike home. I didn't tell Pa about this because he would think I had been teasing her again.

I finished 6th and 7th grade at that little country school near Coleman.

One day my grandma came to visit us in Coleman. We were sitting around the table talking when grandma asked if she could take me home with her to Stanton to attend school because I would get a much better education at the Stanton School. My folks asked me if I wanted to go with grandma and, of course, I

SKETCH OF SHANTIES AT LEONARD SAGE LUMBER CAMP NEAR COLEMAN IN 1901

On the far left, Shanty No. 1 occupied by Supervisor Smith, Shanty No. 2 was the home of Charles and Maggie Sage and our place that Dad built for us where we spent many happy days.

By Tina, age 11.

said, yes. As I looked at my little sister, Ruthie, I said I didn't want to leave her. They said if I wanted to go to school in Stanton I would have to. That was the hardest thing to do. I gave my little angel pin to Ruthie to wear to church and I didn't cry when I left. As I left I was wearing my crepe paper hat I had made at the Coleman country school. The crown and brim both were made from white crepe paper that I had cut into strips crosswise and then braided. I had put a blue ribbon around the crown and let the ends fall down the back in streamers. It looked so pretty, but I guess grandma thought I should have a little better hat for school in Stanton, because she offered to buy me a new one when we got there.

Looking backward in time to the years our family lived in the tar paper three room Shanty #3 near the sawmill in Coleman they were most certainly the happiest days of our lives. We never thought about it then but we lived dangerously. This happy home was a firetrap. It was built of dry native unmatched lumber and covered with very flammable tar soaked paper. It had only one door and was surrounded by slashings. Sometimes it was almost covered with sawdust which served as the best insulation available. A wood burning stove provided the heat and was used for all the cooking. Fuel was free in the form of slab wood from the mill. Some days I remember sparks from the mill engine flying all about. We used to chase them to see who could catch one before it went out. We never did have a fire.

CHAPTER VI

GRADUATION AND THE CERTIFICATE

AFTER BEING IN Stanton for a couple of days I became homesick and wanted to go home but grandma said that after I got acquainted I would be alright — and she was right. I soon forgot my homesickness after I got busy.

That fall of 1903, when I started school in Stanton, my old teacher, Lucinda Gilpin, was still there and kept me from getting too lonesome. Every summer I could take the train back to Coleman and spend my vacation at home. I looked forward to that. The train rides were great. My cousin Maude, was still living with grandma and she helped me out a lot by sewing for me. I remember one of the things she made me was a beautiful plaid blouse and skirt from one of her plaid dresses. I thought it was beautiful.

The big brick building where grandma lived had four floors. The third and fourth floors were the Opera House and balcony. We lived on the second floor. There was a big old stove in the kitchen where I would sit to do my studying at night. Grandma would keep a big pot of soup on the stove — it was so good. On washdays she would get out the copper boiler to use on the stove to boil the clothes before washing. The first floor of the building was a restaurant run by a Mr. and Mrs. Mulholland. After school

I would help them out for ten cents a day. When Mrs. Mulholland needed me she would pound on the ceiling with the broom handle and I would come down. She had a funny way of saying things, too. I remember once she told me to "go rid the fur table." I didn't know what she meant at first but finally interpreted it to mean "clear the table at the far end of the room."

Mrs. Mulholland's husband had a peg leg and he would sit in the front office where he took the money for the customer's meals and played the dulcimer. He made the dulcimer.

I spent five years in school at Stanton, this time, finishing 8th, 9th, 10th, 11th and 12th grades. They had a wonderful curriculum. I had three years of Latin, Creative Writing, Math, Algebra, Geometry, Science and also Shakespeare. How I loved it.

The boys at the Stanton School would tease all the girls and have funny names for them. They called me "Red-White" because of my red hair, which I just hated. Everyone else thought it was pretty. I disliked it so much I wouldn't even wear a red dress! Before I went back to school in Stanton, when I lived in Coleman, I helped the lady in the cook's shanty to earn some money for my schooling. Instead of paying me she gave me some cloth for a dress. When I found out it was red I didn't want it. Another girl in the class always wore a blue coat. Her father, Rance Bearsley, owned the livery stable so the name the boys gave her was "Rance Bearsley's Blue-Blanketed Trotter."

While in high school one of the boys in my class wanted to go steady with me but I said I had to ask my grandma. She said I couldn't, that I had to concentrate on my studies. I was glad she said that because I didn't really want to go with him.

One day in class I remember looking out the window and seeing a lot of smoke. The courthouse was burning! The courthouse was located in Stanton because that was the county seat of Montcalm County. After it burned the supervisors wanted to move the courthouse to Greenville. The people of Stanton protested and fought to keep it where it was and won out. A new courthouse was built on the site of the old one and the seat of Montcalm County remained in Stanton.

The County Normal School had just started, the fall of 1907, when I was in the 11th grade. They lacked a student to fill the

RUINS OF MONTCALM COUNTY, COURTHOUSE

I watched it burn from the schoolhouse window. A bucket brigade was formed but the heat generated by the fire drove them back. What remained was only a shell of masonry. This happened February 15, 1905.

quota so they selected two from high school, me and another girl, to attend the Normal School in addition to high school. They decided to pick the other girl and afterward I was glad they did because I could concentrate on my high school classes and not divide my time between the two. One disappointment, though, was our high school class having to graduate with the County Normal students. We felt it robbed us of our honor of graduating separately. I remember the night of graduation. I wore a dress I had made myself, just for my graduation. It was white trimmed in lace. That was the first thing I had ever made but from then on I made all my own clothes.

The Stanton School, I feel, was a good learning experience and good training for me. It taught me to rely on myself.

After my graduation from high school, the spring of 1908, the County School Commissioner, Eugene Strait, told me if I passed a test that summer I could get a three year teaching certifi-

MY GRADUATION AT STANTON

cate. I took the test, passed it, and got my three year certificate. This entitled me to teach in any of the one room country schools in Michigan.

CHAPTER VII

MY FIRST TEACHING ASSIGNMENTS

MY FIRST YEAR teaching was at Alger, Michigan in Arenac County. It was a one room school with about 30 children. I received $35.00 a month and had to do my own janitor work. (I still have that first contract.) I boarded with Mr. and Mrs. Hartwick about a half mile from the school. Mr. Hartwick was moderator of the school board. I remember the school was near a big woods and it was a lonely place. There were few young people around. Mrs. Hartwick was the largest person I had ever seen—almost 300 lbs. and very tall. They had one little girl, Maggie, who was about eight years old and would walk to school with me every morning. I just loved all of my pupils, they were sweet kids.

I was only eighteen and in the beginning was very lonely. My first trip home was at Thanksgiving and how glad I was to be there. When it came time to go back I cried. I said, "Pa, I can't go back there, it is too lonesome." As I cried, Pa took me by the chin, lifted up my face and looked into my blue eyes and said, "Tina, you'll have to keep your chin up or this old world will snow you right under." I said, "Pa, I will go back but I don't want to." After I got back and into my school work I forgot my lonesomeness.

Mrs. Hartwick boarded lumbermen also, and I had to eat

TEACHERS' CONTRACT.

It is hereby Agreed, By and between the District Board of School District No. _two_ in the Township of _Moffatt_ County of _Arenac_ and State of Michigan, for and on behalf of said District, and _Justina E. White_ of the _City_ of _Standish_ in the County of _Arenac_ and State of Michigan, a legally qualified teacher in said County of _Arenac_ that the said _Justina E. White_ shall teach the _pupils in the_ School of said District for the term of _Eight_ months, commencing on the _1_ day of _Sept_ in the year 190 _8_ for the sum of _$280_ dollars, to be paid as hereinafter specified.

The said _Justina E. White_ hereby agrees to teach said School, for and during the time above mentioned, to keep a correct list of the pupils, and the age of each, attending the said school, and the number of days each pupil is present, and to furnish the Director of said District with a correct copy of the same, at the close of the School, and to faithfully observe and enforce the rules and regulations established by said District Board for the government and management of said School.

The said District Board, on behalf of said District agrees to keep the said School House in good repair, to provide the necessary fuel, and to pay said _Justina E. White_ for her services as teacher of said School for and during the time above mentioned, the sum of _$280_ dollars to be paid as follows _$35 at the end of each month_

Provided, however, that in case the Certificate of said _Justina E. White_ authorizing her to teach, shall expire by limitation, and shall not be immediately renewed, or in case said Certificate shall be suspended or revoked by proper legal authority, then in either case, the said _Justina E. White_ shall not thereafter be entitled to any compensation.

Teacher to do all Janitor work

In Witness Whereof, we have hereunto subscribed our names this _19_ day of _Aug_ A. D. 190 _8_

C. E. Rimmork   _C. W. Hartwick_
Assessor.   Director.

Justina E. White   _Eli Bushnell_
Teacher.   Moderator.

No. 411. W. M. Welch & Company, Chicago.

FIRST TEACHING POSITION

It was at District No. 2 of Moffatt Township Arenac County, more commonly called the Alger School. It was closed and moved from this location in 1960. Note the horse sheds, far left.

REVEREND AND MRS. MYRON DeVOIST

He was instrumental in my conversion at a Summer Camp Meeting on the Taymouth Flats south of Saginaw. He also did the honors at my marriage several years later. He did a good job for me at both events.

breakfast with them. I didn't like that since I was the only girl. I would have preferred eating with the Hartwicks. I remember Mr. Hartwick coming through the kitchen door with big platters of pancakes. They were as big as dinner plates and so delicious. The men saw to it that I got plenty of pancakes. They would try to get me to eat more than one big one.

In the spring I was more than ready to leave and was so happy to be home again. Mr. Hartwick wanted me to stay on another year and would even build on if I would stay so I could have a nice big room of my own. I said I wanted to get another job closer to home.

When I came home that summer, lo and behold! I didn't recognize my Pa because he met me with a new team, two little ponies. He had traded off Mike and Maggie. I felt bad when I didn't see Mike but Pa soothed my fears about him by telling me that the man who bought Mike was putting him out to pasture. The ponies were so cute and the new buggy had a canopy with a little fringe around the top. What a change from a wagon and two work horses to the little buggy and two ponies — I felt so rich riding in it! I later found out they were runaway ponies. One time as we were on our way home they decided to start running. Pa told my sister and me to hang on and not to jump or we would get hurt. He pulled the reins one way and then another trying to get them to slow down until he had the span under control and finally stopped them. Fortunately they never tried that trick again.

The first year I was teaching, my folks moved to Standish. Pa had been selected to fill the pulpit at the Free Methodist Church in Standish, Moore's Junction and Whitefeather. This was his first chance to minister since his calling years before, when a young man.

That summer we went to camp meeting and we visited a campground near Saginaw that had a good memory connected to it, for me. When I was fifteen we had gone to a camp meeting at the same place. While at the meeting I felt I should kneel at the altar because three or four years before that, when I was about twelve, I had torn a book my Pa loved. I had been mad at him for spanking me — I felt I was too old to be spanked — so I tore his book. This had always bothered me, so at that night's service when they asked people to come forward and kneel I felt they were talking to me. I could see this book and felt I had to make it right. I knelt down at that altar and asked the Lord to forgive me. I knew right then the Lord HAD forgiven me. I had to tell Pa, so I went to him and said, "Please forgive me Pa for tearing your book." He said, "Why yes, I do forgive you, I always wondered who tore that book." How good I felt — having that erased from my mind. During this one act my life's direction was completely changed. I always wanted to do the right thing and make the right decisions. This gave me strength from then on because of putting my life in God's hands.

At the time of the camp meetings, my folks would invite the District Elders home for the district meetings and for dinner. We girls would all help Ma. She would cook the most delicious

MY SECOND SCHOOL

Pupils at the East Twining School. They kept me busy for the years 1910–11. I am top center, fourth from the left.

chicken dinner and we would use our white tablecloth and be on our best behavior. Two of our favorite ministers that came to our home were Rev. DeVoist and Rev. Porterfield. (Coincidently, Rev. Porterfield's great-nephew is the manager of Briarwood Manor where I am now living.)

Another one of the ministers who attended the camp meetings was a Chippewa Indian and we would listen to him pray in the Chippewa language. He was married to a white woman named Lillian. He had taken the white name of Moses Smith. They lived at Edwards, near West Branch. We became friends and were invited to their new log home they had built on a big

A HANDSOME SWAIN

Robert Hamilton, who I left behind after teaching two years at the East Twining School, was the brother of my best friend, Mildred. He had a fast horse and a nice buggy. We were thankful neither could talk! But the birds sang to us from the rail fences.

lake. They liked to fish and we would enjoy the fish and fishing when we visited them.

They had an organ in their little house that they let me play. I had learned to play by ear and I remember the fun we had singing while I played. One of the songs we all loved was called "Redwing."

We learned a lot from the Indians; how to make a fire and cook over it and how to make Indian bread. It was baked on a flat stone in front of the fire. That bread was so good, the best ever.

During one summer vacation when Pa, Mildred, Mary and I went berry picking (we usually went for a few days and camped out) one of our horses got away and we went looking for him about dark. We finally found him in a swampy area, but couldn't find our way out. In the morning some Indians came, also picking berries, heard us and came to the rescue. Another time when we were camping Indian dogs were sniffing around our camp for food and came into the tent. We couldn't get them out because they would only respond to Indian commands. Finally we managed to solve the problem after we learned "a-wiska-jing" meant "get out of here!"

The fall of 1909, my second year of teaching, was at the East Twining School near Twining, Michigan. It also was a one room school but had about fifty children from beginners through the 8th grade, so I received better pay. (I still have that contract, too.)

I found a boarding place at a Mr. and Mrs. Compton's about a half mile from school. They lived in a little log house. I liked the Comptons very much, but their son, L.D., was a pain in the neck. He was much older than I and loved to tease me. The first Sunday I was there he asked me to go for a buggy ride and get

BERRY PICKERS

This was a blackberry picking party where there were so many of us we could not get lost. The mosquitos were big here. I took the picture.

IN A DANISH SETTLEMENT

The Gowen School was my next assignment. There I found a superior group of students. I am again in the top row, fourth from the left.

acquainted with the countryside. I accepted. After that he told everyone I was his girlfriend. Well, when I heard that, I told him I would not go for a ride again, I was not his girlfriend and never would be. Still he didn't stop teasing me. For example, when we were at the table and I would ask him to please pass the butter he would shove it so my thumb would go into the butter. Another favorite trick of his was to come along when I was ironing and grab my clothes off the ironing board. One day I was pressing pleats in my skirt and I had some water to sprinkle on the pleats for steam. L.D. came along, grabbed my skirt off the board and started flipping water on me. I got so mad and we finally ended up in the yard throwing water at each other. I also didn't like the

THE MORTENSEN HOME

I boarded here while teaching at Gowen and got fat on Mrs. Mortensen's cooking. The house was even loaded with gingerbread on the outside.

way he would swear, so I told his mother I was moving. She said she would talk to L.D. about his teasing and swearing. She persuaded me to stay by straightening out her son and I finished out the year at the Comptons.

At Twining, when I walked to school, the birds would follow me along the fence and sing to me. One day L.D. wanted to take me to school. I didn't want to go with him so I told him the meadowlarks and bob-o-links would miss me. That was the best excuse I could come up with.

That year at Twining there were more young people around so I didn't get so lonesome as I had at Alger. There was one young man who paid attention to me. He was two years older than I, so handsome and a good person, too. He helped me with my luggage when I got there and took me to the Comptons. His name was Robert Hamilton. I admired him very much. He helped me all that year, especially with the janitor duties around the school. Robert wanted to marry me. Though I admired him and liked

CLEANUP CREW AT HAYNES

A two room school following the annual Christmas Exercises. The tall man in the corner was an eighth grade winter term student. Young country school teachers usually had lots of volunteers to do their odd jobs. I am on the left.

him I was not ready to marry. He came along too soon or was not patient enough. I remember the day we said good-bye, standing by the fence with the meadowlarks singing so sweetly. He had me almost persuaded but looking back now I feel I made the right decision. Robert's sister, Mildred, was a fine person and my best friend while at East Twining.

The children at Twining were more advanced than the children at Alger. One of the things I loved about teaching was the creativity and the music. One of the school plays we put on was called "Fun on the Podunk Limited." The word "Podunk" was a word I picked up from my family conversations. The children pretended they were at the railway station and would be arriving and departing on the train. They made all the scenery themselves. They made the coach from old boards and painted it to look just like a railroad coach. How the parents loved that play!

I liked it so well at the East Twining School that I taught

EVA BELLE CLARK

Eva (on the right) with whom I shared teaching duties at Haynes. I do not know why we looked so worldly.

MY MOTHER'S QUINTETTE

She nurtured us so tenderly while Pa was our disciplinarian and advisor. They were wonderful parents. The five of us are the result of their handiwork. L to R. (Top) Mary, Mildred & Ruth (Bottom) Grace & Justina.

there a second year. When it came time to say good-bye, after my two years, I went to West Branch to spend the summer at home. (My folks had moved to West Branch after three years at Standish. Pa was preaching at West Branch, Campbells Corners and Edwards.) Grace was home, too, after teaching one year at the Twining school in town.

That fall my folks moved back to Stanton because my grandmother needed them. My three year teaching certificate had expired so I went back to Stanton and took a test and received another three year teaching certificate. I wanted to keep teaching

SODA JERK

Victor Smith — working in the soda fountain of Charles Carothers, Stanton while not working in the Smith Brothers Grocery and soon to be the breaker up of the White Quintette.

because I was saving my money so I could go to college and also to help Grace through college at Ferris Institute.

My next school was in Montcalm County in the Danish settlement school near Gowen. There were only twenty children and I was receiving about $50.00 a month then. The Danish people are such neat clean people and how they can cook! I boarded with the Mortensen's and each day when I would come home from school Mrs. Mortensen would have Danish rolls and coffee for me. (She kept the coffee pot going all day long.) I weighed more then than at any time in my life.

I taught at the school at Gowen for just one year and then found another school five miles from Stanton. It was called the

ALMOST A CITY

Sometimes, if the weather was good I would walk the five miles from my boarding place near Gowen on Friday nights to see my folks and other friends in Stanton.

Haynes School and was a big change for me. It was two rooms and I taught 5th through 10th grades. Beginners and first through fourth grades were taught by a Marian Evans. We got along fine and I admired her so much that I promised her when I got married if I had a little girl I would name her Marian. Though I had just a few pupils I was teaching subjects I wanted to brush up on, so it was a big help to me. Sometimes on Friday nights I would walk the five miles home to Stanton, which was good for me.

It was about this time that I met Victor Smith again, the same boy who had wanted to take me home from the Baptist Church when I was about ten. Wow! What a change. He was tall and handsome, his eyes just sparkled and he had dimples when he smiled. I thought, "My, is that little Victor Smith?" I could hardly believe my eyes. He was about one and one-half years younger than I but he seemed much older than his age—so we were just

CONFIDENT YOUNG MAN

*A confident young man with a wasp waisted
school marm during their courting days — or
daze. He was 22. I was 24. It was Victor.*

about right. He was going with another girl at the time but after
we met again he lost all interest in her and we started going
together. I knew I was a gone gosling!

I taught two years at the Haynes School and it seemed my
vision of going to college was fading. It was such a struggle to get
enough money because I was helping Grace get through Ferris.
Also, Mr. Smith was looking awful good to me. I did not want to
lose him.

Victor asked me to marry him before he was to enlist in the
War. I told him I would, but I wanted to go to college first. He
surprised me so when he said, "Well, we'll just go to college

together. I have enough money saved for both of us to go." Victor was very thrifty and had saved his money he earned working with his brothers in the Smith Brothers Grocery on Main Street in Stanton. It was right across from grandma's old hotel. I said I would marry him and we would go to college together.

Chapter VIII

MARRIAGE, TRAGEDY AND COLLEGE

WE WERE MARRIED on September 15, 1914 in the Free Methodist Church parsonage in Owosso by Rev. Myron DeVoist. I had met the DeVoists at camp meetings and liked them so well I wanted him to marry us. Since my Grandma and Grandpa Sage lived in Corunna, near Owosso, Grandpa Sage and my sister, Grace, signed our marriage certificate. We had just a small wedding. My cousin, Will Cooper and Grace were the attendants. They and Grandpa Sage were the only ones attending. Grandma Sage was busy at home getting a nice dinner ready for us.

Up until now I have told you mostly about my Grandma and Grandpa White because we were living with them while I was growing up and while I attended high school. We were also close to Grandma and Grandpa Sage. They were such wonderful people. Grandma Sage was a good cook and a sweet, dear person. She especially loved children and they loved her. At her funeral a whole row of children sat behind the pallbearers as a tribute to their love for her.

One of the things I remember about grandma, as a child, was her entertaining us with a "peek box." In a cardboard box she would fashion a room-setting in miniature that she would make

MR. AND MRS. VICTOR H. SMITH

September 15, 1914

from scraps of material and odds and ends and furnish it down to
the last detail. Then she would put tissue paper over the top and
cut a "peek" hole in it. She would then make covers of different
color tissue paper so when the light filtered through the paper it
would cast a different glow on the little room. She was creative
and I think I inherited this trait from her which served me well in
my years of teaching.

After Victor and I were married we went back to Grandma
and Grandpa Sage's home for our wedding dinner. Grandma had
prepared a delicious meal. After dinner we went to Stanton to
Victor's parents to stay a few days before taking our wedding trip.
Victor's brother, as a joke, had decorated our room with all kinds

of "pictures." One of them, I remember, was a pair of big eyes and ears looking down from the ceiling over our bed. The rascal!

We were there a few days before leaving for a trip to Milwaukee going across Lake Michigan from Grand Haven on a steamship. Victor had worked as a shipping clerk at the steamship line in Milwaukee before going in with his brothers in the grocery business and he wanted me to see Milwaukee. We had a wonderful time. Victor had a brand new navy blue suit and I, too, had a navy suit. With it I wore a navy blue hat with a lining of white satin. It certainly complimented my long red hair.

When we returned to Stanton, after our honeymoon, we stayed with Victor's parents again for about six months. Then we rented the Old Gilpin house (Lucinda's parents old home) for about a year. In the meantime, my folks had purchased a house across from the new hotel in Stanton and were preparing the downstairs for us. They lived upstairs. It was built on the side of a hill so there were no windows in the back. However, there were beautiful windows in the front and I made all of the curtains for them. I still have one of the curtains, because I had done so much handwork on them.

During the first six months when we were still with Victor's parents I found out I was pregnant, but after only three months I lost the baby. Not realizing how hard on me it would be, I had done a lot of heavy cleaning and lifting. I even helped grandma move her piano. I feel all this lifting probably caused me to lose the baby. The doctor thought it was a little boy and I felt so sorry, but nothing could be done.

We moved into the apartment at Pa and Ma's in 1915. We were happy there. We bought a brand new Kalamazoo heating stove that burned hard coal. We would sit in front of the stove on cold winter nights looking at the blue flames through the isinglass windows and were as "snug as bugs in a rug." The coal scuttle always had lots of coal in it nearby.

One night I said, "Victor, when are we going to college?" He said that as soon as I was well enough, and that he had been saving some more money for college. Before I knew it, I was pregnant again. This time it was different. I was healthy and carried the baby to full term, thinking all the while it was a little girl. I spent the winter making little clothes for a baby girl and would lay them out on the bed just picturing her in them. I thought we would just take her with us to college — I wasn't going to give up.

When the time came for her birth, the last week in February, I was ill for three days. I had a hard time in labor. She should have been born on leap year day, February 29th, but I struggled so long they finally had to take her on March 1, 1916. She was born dead. How devastated I felt. My sister, Grace, who had become a nurse, was with me and she did everything she could. They all worked hard over the baby but they couldn't save her. How sad Victor and I were. I cried and mourned for that baby all summer. My Pa would come down and try to comfort me, but to no avail. Finally, Victor said, "You are not going to grieve anymore, we are going to college now." That helped to cheer me up. So we packed our belongings, closed our apartment and left in the early fall for college — finally!

We enrolled in a small Free Methodist College in Evansville, Wisconsin. My cousin, Dr. Fred E. Bennett, was the history teacher and helped us get settled in a nice apartment he had arranged for us on campus.

The school needed a Dean of Boys, so they chose Victor. The school, being small, had only about 20 or 25 boys. Victor was apprehensive about handling the job but Fred and Dr. R. R. Blews, the President of the college, helped him get started and were very reassuring and so nice to him. Victor also enrolled in History and English classes in addition to his duties as Dean of Boys. I enrolled in History of Western Europe (that Fred taught), English and Creative Writing, French and Piano. I loved it so much that even with my heavy schedule I maintained all A's. Together we liked it so well there it helped to ease our grief over losing our baby girl.

We finished out the year at school but the war was on and Victor felt he had to enlist. Most of the single men were drafted. His brother, Carl, had already enlisted and gone overseas. We moved into his house while he was gone and then I stayed on there, by myself, after Victor went to war. (I had signed the papers so he could enlist.)

To keep busy after Victor left, I worked at Smith Brothers Grocery and for the Red Cross rolling bandages. I can still see all

| A VOLUNTEER | ON FURLOUGH |

Victor responded to the call. He fig- ured it was his duty. He is shown here as a green recruit in his new G.I. World War I uniform.

Victor enlisted during World War I. I took his place in the Grocery and worked as a Red Cross Volunteer. It was a lonesome time for both of us.

the boys lined up to leave. The women would go down to the train station to see them off and we would sing "There's a Long, Long Trail A Winding." It was so sad to say good-bye. When Victor enlisted in 1917, there was only one year left of the war but in 1918 the flu epidemic hit. Victor was stricken with it and had to stay another three months after the war ended, until he was well enough to come home.

In the meantime, when the war ended, there was a big celebration in Stanton. A parade was planned with floats and the Stanton Marine Band, led by Mr. John Hartman. What a celebration! Everyone was banging on pots and pans and singing. I rode on a float behind the marching Marine Band. All of us on the float wore red Eton jackets, white blouses and long blue skirts. We were such a happy bunch. There were about 25 or 30 of us clapping and singing. Everyone was so glad the war was over. I shall never forget this. The old-timers said it was the greatest celebration ever held in Stanton.

CHAPTER IX

SECURING OUR FAMILY

AFTER THE WAR Victor sold his share of the Smith Brothers Grocery business back to his two brothers and we decided to move to Flint. Ma and Pa had moved to Flint right before we did and lived on Indiana Avenue. We lived with Aunt Hattie for awhile after coming to Flint because she had room for us. We joined the Pilgrim Holiness Church of Flint which later merged with the First Wesleyan Church on Davison Road. While living at Aunt Hattie's I became pregnant with Vernon John. He was born in Hurley Hospital May 4, 1920. In the meantime, we had a little bungalow built at 610 Bishop Avenue.

That summer we had a terrible time with the baby, he was sick all summer. We took him to a baby doctor, Dr. Jickling, and he found that Vernon was in the last stages of starvation. I was having so much difficulty trying to nurse him because he would just cry. When Dr. Jickling found out Carrie Morey was nursing her baby, he asked if she would also nurse mine. So along with my cousin nursing Vernon and a good formula Dr. Jickling had made up, Vernon soon started gaining but was nine months old before he finally quit crying. Years later, when he went into the service, the doctor discovered he had suffered a broken rib when he was a baby. We believe this accounted for his crying. He was in pain.

When Vernon was only a little over six months old I found I

A HOME OF OUR OWN

Our own home on Bishop Avenue in Flint was built especially for us. There were plenty of jobs, good churches and schools, and it was almost in the country.

FAMILY PLACE

Our home at 1702 Broadway in Flint was large enough to raise a family and it was closer to the school. We had made a good swap.

OUR LITTLE BOYS

Vernon, age 4, Victor, Jr., 4 mos., and Robert, almost 3 yrs. old. Taken in the spring of 1924.

was pregnant again. I was worried that we would have problems with the new baby also. Robert Nathan was born at home on August 13, 1921 (15 months after Vernon) and was in perfect health. We were so thankful. He was the sweetest little doll!

About this time we had a chance to buy a place close to our folks and closer to the school for our boys. We moved into a larger home at 1702 Broadway. While living there we had another baby boy, born on January 4, 1924 and named him Victor Henry Smith, Jr. Now we had our hands full with three babies.

Victor, Jr. was born at home, too, and I remember Vernon coming up to the bed, looking at the baby and saying, "Mama, weigh him up again and mark him down as Jimmie." He didn't think he should be named the same as his father. You never knew

A WAGON FULL

A wagon full of responsibility but worth every bit of it when this photo was taken in 1924. L to R: Vernon, 4 years, Bobby, 3, and Baby Victor Jr., 7 months.

what Vernon was going to say. One day, at the store, a man came in with a full beard. Vernon had never seen a beard before, so after staring at him, he pointed his finger at his beard and said, "Is that really hair?"

During this period I continued my education, taking correspondence courses and attending three summer sessions at Central Michigan University at Mt. Pleasant. In 1931, when the boys were seven, nine, and eleven, I renewed my teaching certificate for life.

MY SWEET LITTLE BOYS

L to R: Bob, Victor Jr, and Vernon. Notice that they were wearing three different styles of shoes. That was my boys' choice and they followed that pattern throughout their lives.

BATH SCHOOL DISASTER

38 children and teachers were killed by a dynamite exploison set off by a deranged local farmer, Andrew Kehoe, who also killed his own family, burned his farm buildings and finally shot himself. We took the boys, Father, and other family members and went to the site like hundreds of other people. As usual, I took my box camera along and recorded the destruction wrought by the forces of evil. May 17, 1927. Total deaths numbered 45.

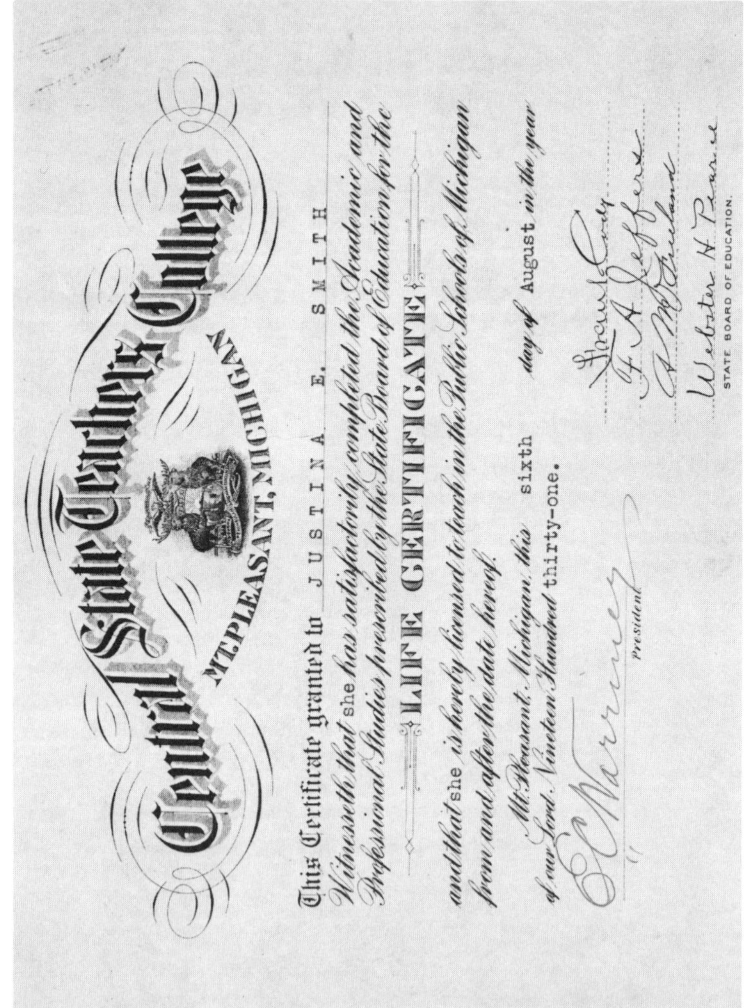

LIFE CERTIFICATE

I stuck to teaching like a puppy to a root for twenty-one years until I earned this privilege.

CHAPTER X

MICHIGAN THE BEAUTIFUL

I N 1929, WHILE attending Central Michigan University that summer, Victor and I and our three small boys took a trip by car to the Upper Peninsula of Michigan and many points in between. This is an account of that unforgettable trip which I also used as one of my writing assignments.

We left Flint early one Wednesday morning, after having spent nearly half the night packing and fastening luggage on our Chevrolet, which was certainly loaded with bedding, eats, tent, etc. We ate a pancake breakfast in Owosso, then on to Grand Rapids, Grand Haven and north along the shore until dusk began to overtake us. We pulled into Pentwater but it was such a dirty sandy beach with no camping ground that I simply refused to stay, so we went on to Ludington and found a fine camping spot on the velvety green grass among the trees in Water Works Park. We were tired and glad to roll into our beds. We had stopped in Muskegon, and although the stores were closed, we stuck around Sears Roebuck & Company Store and begged until they let us in. We just simply had to buy a bed. We purchased a nice little folding one with springs and it was very comfortable. The boys slept on the ground with a waterproof mattress. Next morning it was bright and breezy.

THE TOURISTS

This picture taken a few Sundays before we started out on our Michigan excursion.

ROUGHING IT

Here are some one-night-stand neighbors from Illinois who traveled a little better than we did — but comparable.

Lake Michigan was pounding and tossing little white crests of foam which we could easily see from our camp. She was inviting us to follow her shoreline. We got everything packed after cooking breakfast and eating in the open, and waited just long enough for Victor to take a snapshot of me dressed in my knickers and sweater with my field glasses strapped over my shoulder.

We followed the shoreline as much as possible, passing through Manistee, past beautiful Portage Lake, Arcadia, Frankfort, around the west end of beautiful Crystal Lake, near Beulah, Michigan (where the annual smelt run draws crowds from all over the state), then north to Glen Haven. We found a wonderful state park among the tall, stately pines and white birches. This camp is about two miles from Glen Lake, called the second most beautiful lake in the world. It lies in a depression bounded on the east and north by wooded shores and on the west by great sand dunes that rise high against the sky, forming a great ridge or barrier between Glen Lake and Lake Michigan which lies about three miles to the west. From the top of these dunes one can get a wonderful view of Glen Lake nestled among the trees, like a sparkling jewel in its setting of green.

Never will I forget the second evening we spent at Glen Lake. We climbed the east shore to a place called Lookout Point. The sun was just setting, tinting the sky with soft colors that blended in a harmony of rose, apple green and violet. Below, possibly three hundred feet from our vantage point, we could see practically all of the lake, lying serene and placid like a great mirror, reflecting the colors of the sunset. Fringing its shores were little evergreen trees and here and there in the more cleared spaces we could see houses and roads that looked so small because of the distance. It seemed like a fairyland. There were several boats on the lake, most of them anchored for fishing. It was such a quiet, restful place. We waited until the great "red" sun had dipped down behind the wooded slopes and rolling sand dunes that bound the shores of old Lake Michigan until it was lost to our view. The air was getting cooler now and the sunset colors were merging into darker tones, so we hastened down from Lookout Point, taking a peep into a deep dark woods by way of a little path that branched off from the main one. It was cool and mossy smelling but darkness was coming so we retraced our steps to the main path and were soon in the car and on our way back to the snug little tent.

Next morning we arose quite early for we were planning to visit the sand dunes that day. It was nice and clear and there was quite a breeze blowing. We reached a place at the foot of the dunes where some people by the name of F. H. Dillor from 1108 Spruce Street, Winnetka, Illinois had a nice cottage about 200 feet from the foot of the dunes. He said at the rate that the sand shifted each year, in a little over 100 years the place where his cottage, grove and flower gardens were, would be completely covered by sand.

We started for the huge pile of sand and such fun it was climbing up and sliding back now and then, but we finally reached the top. We did not know at that time that it was dangerous, for tons of sand have been known to take a sudden slide and bury people. From the top we could see for miles, Glen Lake lying below and blue hills to the north, while to the west, stretching as far as the eye could see, was the blue expanse of Lake Michigan. We sat down to rest, had our picture taken on the ridge of the dune, then proceeded to plod our way across this desert toward Lake Michigan. The dune we were on is called Sleeping Bear, and there is an Indian legend that once a mother bear swam across Lake Michigan, from the Wisconsin shore, with her two small cubs, but before reaching the shore the two baby bears grew tired and drowned. After the mother reached land she stretched out, resting her head on her paws, but her cubs had turned into two islands, the Manitous, which can plainly be seen from shore. The dune on the Michigan shore is shaped like a huge bear, sleeping and waiting for the two cubs who never came and that is why it is called Sleeping Bear Dune.

The little village of Glen Haven lies just to the north of it and it was near this village that we camped in the lovely state park where there are stoves, a little store and many other conveniences.

We waded until our shoes were filled with sand, (pure white sand) then we took them off. The boys sure enjoyed it but before we reached the Lake Michigan Shore, I grew too tired to go on, sat down on a big pile of sand and dry weeds and had my picture taken with the two islands lying out in the blue haze, as a background. Now and then we could see another tourist or two plodding along with the aid of a staff. The dune is not perfectly level but ridged and rippled by winds. We would climb to the top of a ridge and think it was only a short distance to the lake. By the time we reached one ridge we found it was farther than we expected so we finally retraced our steps. The boys had great fun sliding down the ridges of shifting sand and by the time we reached vegetation again we were surely a "sandy" bunch of people. It was in our teeth, our hair and down our backs, for we had spent about a half day on the dune and the wind was blowing hard. Little Victor was sure a little "brick", for he, being shorter than the rest, got the full blast of the blowing sand in his face. I took a picture of Victor and the boys standing beside some half-buried, scrubby trees that had been overtaken by the shifting sand. The bark was nearly ground from them. They were the only trees we saw and it is said that whole forests have been buried underneath the dunes. Now and then a dry stub can be seen protruding through the sand on the windward side of the dune.

That evening, after we were all cleaned up and had eaten a good dinner, we went to the little village of Glen Haven, bought some post card pictures of the dunes and Glen Lake and mailed them to our friends. We were all tired, but happy, for we were seeing some of the wonders, beauties and secrets of this wonderful world God has made. We read about these things but never can realize their grandeur until we see them for ourselves.

The next morning, after a refreshing sleep, we began to pack up, ready to start on north although we hated to leave this beautiful place. We bade good-bye to our brief neighbors, a nice couple, who had their invalid son with them, trying to nurse him back to health in the great out-of-doors.

We drove through Day's Forest Reserve then out to the main highway. We followed the shore as much as possible, via M 22, through Leland (the home of a Mt. Pleasant classmate), through Northport and around by Sutton's Bay. Here we saw many Indian homes and an Indian Village. We passed beautiful Lake Leelenau and through some very pretty hilly country. We found good concrete roads and reached Traverse City quite late in the evening, camping in the city tourist camp which was a nice level park

THE SAND DUNES

These mountains of small grains of sand were now behind us but their memory will always remain. Here we are trying to climb one, in vain.

AN OLD STEAMER

A ferry boat from Beaver Island comes in off the big water, preparing to dock at Charlevoix.

filled with tall trees and right on the shore of the west part of Grand Traverse Bay. There were many campers here and we met some people next morning from St. Louis, Michigan. We visited for quite awhile, so got rather a late start. It began misting a little during the forenoon but we were dry and our waterproof covers kept our luggage dry. We passed around the east side of Grand Traverse Bay, then north via US 31, through Elk Rapids, from where we could see lovely Elk Lake and a little farther north, beautiful blue Torch Lake that stretches for miles although we could see it only in glimpses from the main highway. We passed through Charlevoix, a fine city where the shops are full of tourists buying curios. By the time we reached Petoskey it was raining quite hard but we stopped, bought some hamburg, buns, tomatoes, cookies and a few other eats for the boys, then proceeded toward Harbor Springs. Petoskey is also a pretty place, full of tourists that day and the shop windows were full of Indian baskets, beaded articles, etc. We followed Little Traverse Bay — a lovely drive along the waterfront — the shores lined with cottages practically all the way with pretty names such as Lullwater, Dun Workin and Ken-Tuck-You-In. We passed through Bay View and finally reached Harbor Springs just as it began pouring. We pulled into the tourist camp under some heavy sheltering trees, got out our little stove and I made hamburgers and coffee while the rain came dripping down over our food, but not daunting our spirits. This is part of the tourist's life and the rain must be taken along with the sunshine. We laughed and were happy watching the boys grab a hamburg bun (and they could eat plenty of them) and run under a long shed to eat out of the rain. We had on our raincoats so stuck it out until everything was picked up, packed and ready to move on again. It was about 2 P.M. now, and we went to Uncle Jim's home on the top of the bluff overlooking the harbor, hoping to find him home and sure enough, he was reading the paper, having come home from his barbershop to spend the noon hour. Aunt Winnifred and her niece from Saginaw, who was visiting her, were out in the neat little kitchen. Were they surprised? I'll say so. We visited and had a jolly half hour while the rain came gently down, then we bade good-bye although they wanted us to stay.

We set out for Mackinaw City, taking the Shore Road. Let

HARBOR SPRINGS YESTERDAY

Uncle Lemuel and Uncle Jim White (left to right) in the door of their Barber Shop while a variety of village hang-a-bouts look on.

OUR BIG CATCH

We had a fish apiece and you can nearly see them. We are with new friends we met on the trail.

me say right here that this drive is one of the prettiest I have ever been on. The road winds through the woods and now and then one gets a glimpse of Lake Michigan on the left, deep, blue and beautiful. This day it was covered with little whitecaps, but the sky began to clear and we got out of the car to peek down from the high cliff we were on, to a little Indian village nestled among the trees on the shore. All was quiet except the pounding lake. Finally we saw an Indian walking on the beach and soon some Indian children came out to play and wave their hands at us high above. I took my field glasses and could see their gardens. A little weather-beaten church with a cross on top was at one end of the settlement. We proceeded on through Cross Village, a really historic old place where an early settlement was made and where Father Marquette labored among the Indians. For many years, a huge cross marked the historic site of Cross Village.

From here we left the shoreline and proceeded east to Levering, a small town where I met an old roommate of mine from Mt. Pleasant by the name of Lela Schmalgried. We visited awhile then started due north on US 31, making a jog around Carp Lake and on north toward Mackinaw City. The air seemed so much fresher and purer here. The sun was shining by now and it was getting toward late afternoon so we hurried on eager to make the ferry before nightfall. When we reached Mackinaw City we beheld the broad expanse of Lake Michigan to our left, Lake Huron to our right and the beautiful Straits of Mackinaw connecting the two. A little to the northeast was Mackinac Island rising quite abruptly from the water, and toward the northwest we could see the dim outline of St. Ignace and a bit of the Upper Peninsula enveloped in the purple haze of a fast gathering twilight. Sea gulls were soaring about and getting ready to settle down on the piers for the night. A long line of traffic was waiting for the ferry as we swung in, creeping along a few feet each time the boat took on an automobile. After about an hour we were safe inside the ferry. We put on our coats as it was very cool and went up on deck. The sun had set, still it was a very pretty sight just the same. Little lights were twinkling everywhere on shore. A passenger steamer, on its way from Mackinac Island, went past us with lights all aglow. There was an exchange of whistles as the two came abreast. The Lower Peninsula and the lights from Mackinaw City gradually faded in the distance and after about, what seemed to be, an hour the Upper Peninsula and lights of St. Ignace came plainly into view. Soon we were on solid ground again and in our auto and out looking for a camping place. We soon found one on the southwest edge of town. It was a state park full of the nicest evergreen trees I have ever seen in my life. The air was invigorating. First, I proceeded to get something warm to eat as we had only had a cold bite of food since eating our hamburgers in Harbor Springs. Victor lit our nice old friend, the gasoline lantern, put up the tent and after we had eaten I fixed the beds and we all rolled in for a good nights rest. Next morning the sun was bright and beautiful so I took some pictures while we were eating breakfast. The children ran to play on the slides and swings in the park after breakfast and I tidied everything up while Victor serviced the car. We got under motion and made a tour of inspection, visiting Castle Rock and the Rabbits Back, a high rise of shoreline from which one can see many islands lying to the right and left and the dim outline of the Lower Peninsula, lake freighters steaming by and sea gulls circling above. We took some pictures from the top of this high rise and spent quite some time enjoying the grandeur of it all. The evergreens were thick all about. With the aid of field glasses we could see dwellings in little clearings and here and there a road, like a ribbon running through the green.

The lady who kept the little resort at the foot of the Rabbits Back told us many interesting stories of the history of this place. She said the Indians had used the Rabbits Back as a signal station for generations. They would use pitch flares for signals in time of war.

On the way back we went through the Evergreen Shore Drive.

We stopped in Indian Village, a place in the city of St. Ignace where there are birch bark houses, wigwams etc. and where Indian baskets, trinkets and curios are sold. The Indians make most of these. The places were permeated with the odor of sweet grass. We bought some souvenirs and I took a picture of the boys standing in front of the little birch bark house made by the Moses Brothers, called the most powerful Indians of the north.

This little house was wired and lighted. Little wigwams and other scenes were carved on the birch bark inside.

We stayed one more night in St. Ignace then packed and left quite early next morning for the northwest, going over a paved road that stretched for miles through forests. There were many lonely stretches that had previously been burned over. For miles we never met a car or saw a human being. We went through Rexton, Garnet and to Newberry, a very pretty, clean town, where a large hospital is located. From here we proceeded through Seney and Shingleton and on toward Munising. The country of evergreen forests and rolling hills were very beautiful. There were many boulders and glacial rocks especially around Garnet. We came out on top of a big hill and there was Munising lying below in the harbor and just across a little bay was Grand Island like a big green jewel set in beautiful, big, blue Lake Superior. This was our first glimpse of Superior and we were thrilled! It stretched away so deep, cold and sparkling. Some fleecy clouds were hanging low in the far northwest and the sun was just setting, tinting these clouds with soft colors that reflected on the bosom of the lake. There was a long golden path that led straight toward the sun. We began to look for a camp and there, right at a bend in the road at the top of the hill, was a wonderfully clean grove where many white tents were pitched. Over the drive was an archway which read "Policed Camp," so we drove in and soon a young man came running up to show us where to set up. The camp was full so we had to take about the only place left which was way back at the edge of a big dark woods. It was cold and getting dark so we had to hurry and get things ready for nightfall. We did not like the actions of the young man who seemed too eager to help and inspect our luggage. In a little while a young girl told us to sign a ledger which her father kept, for it was a pay camp. Then she warned us against the young fellow, after he had gone to help another tourist, telling us to hang on to any valuables as he was not hired to do the work there but had been hanging around while her father was away. She said he had been known to steal. We thanked her and kept our eyes open the rest of that evening, in fact all night we were rather scared, being so close to the dense woods, but the guard came and assured us that he would keep a special watch over our tent as he was on duty every night. He ordered the fellow to leave camp and never come back.

We had heard there were many pretty waterfalls around Munising, so were anxious to start out the next day. In the morning I cleaned some huckleberries which we had picked beside the road on our trip the day before through the long stretches of burned over timber lands. They had a wild tang and tasted good. We had slept rather cold that night, for old Lake Superior certainly affects the atmosphere, so we went downtown and bought another wool blanket and I was surely glad that I had sense enough to bring along our flannel sleeping garments.

When everything was set and the tent tied up, we were ready to start our days sightseeing. The coffee, bacon, toast and huckleberries were good out-of-doors in the crisp cool morning air. This breakfast gave us a good start for the day. My, how the eats would disappear when those hungry boys got after them and I wasn't far behind either.

We went to Tannery Falls first which was on the east edge of the town. A stream came tumbling and gurgling by and finally reached the edge of a big high rock ledge where it tumbled over the edge and to the rocks below finding its outlet under logs and through ferns and on through the woods. It was very pretty there and so cool. We walked behind the falls and sat for quite awhile on a big stone at the bottom watching the water tumble from high above. We took some pictures here, too, and picked some of the pretty ferns from the rock ledge.

We also visited Wagner Falls which was such a pretty waterfall, rushing down through the ledges, under logs and around the bends in this rustic place. The boys climbed out on a log right over the falls and I took their picture although it was rather dark and shady. They liked to watch the water bubble, splash and ripple as it was tossed over the stones and around in little eddies, making a musical sound that is so restful to those who are accustomed to the brash city noises.

From here we traveled quite a distance north and east, following signs that pointed "This way to Miner's Falls, Miner's Castle and the Pictured Rocks." Soon we came to a sign that pointed east of the main road. We followed it, driving in as far as we could to a little clearing where we parked our car. From here we took a path through the woods for over one-half mile past some men who were lumbering. Over logs and around bends we continued until we finally heard a rush of water. We came to the edge of a deep ravine down the side of which plunged Miner's Falls. It was a sight worth the effort we had made to reach it. To get to the foot of the falls we had to climb down a sort of stairway made of poles imbedded in the ravine with a railing along one side. The steps numbered one hundred and ninety. One had to be pretty sure of his footing. I was glad I had worn my knickers and I carried a staff that someone had left at the clearing where we parked. This was a pretty strenuous life and I developed pleurisy for most of the remainder of this trip. I did not want to miss any of the sights and believe me, I didn't. Every place we visited was historic and inspiring.

Here at Munising, "Stood the Wigwam of Nakomis, daughter of the moon" and grandmother of Hiawatha. It was here that Longfellow was inspired.

On the way back we met three dapper looking young men wearing racoon coats and I thought to myself, boys you'll shed those coats before you get to the foot of the falls. I do not believe they went way down in the ravine for in a little while they came back, climbed into their roadster and drove away.

From the main road we started out for the Pictured Rocks and Miner's Castle which was about five miles farther north. It was a dirt road that was rather rough and meandered through the woods practically all the way. Finally we reached the end of this road, where in a clearing, several cars were parked and some people were eating their lunch. We were hungry, so ate our lunch first, then started down the path that led toward Lake Superior's shore. We were high up, for at this point the lake is bounded by high sandstone cliffs that rise abruptly in many places hundreds of feet above the water and at this point they are known as the Pictured Rocks, because of the varied colors of the strata found in the sandstone. These colors glisten in the sun and are a wonderful sight. The boys were eager to run down alone in some of the steepest places, so we hung on to them and made them keep to the path which turned to the left and out onto a jutting promontory of solid rock which rose high into the air hundreds of feet above the tumbling, splashing, green water below. This abutment of rock is known as Miner's Castle and it is a great castle indeed; as if it were a lookout tower from which one could see for many miles. The path leading to it is rather narrow and there is no railing, so I hung onto the boys, for one misstep would dash them over to the rocks and the swirling waters below. Bobby dropped a pine cone near the edge and wanted to retrieve it. No way would we let him do it. It was a wonderful view from this point. Words fail to describe it! To our right lay the shoreline curving toward the northeast. The colors of the Pictured Rocks and Cambrian sandstone, probably over 100 million years old, gleamed softly in the sun and were topped by verdant forests of evergreens and birches. To our left, lying in a small sheltered bay in the finest land-locked harbor on the Great Lakes was the little city of Munising with rising hills and forest in its background. Across from the mouth of the harbor Grande Island lay, green and beautiful. This island is a resting place for the wealthy. The pictured rocks line the shore most of the way and in many places the waves have washed out alcoves in the sandstone that could be called caves. They say many of these places are carved with Indian picture writing of the long ago when native Americans were masters of this region. To the east, north and west, as far as the eye could see, the deep, blue, cold, sparkling waters of Lake Superior touch the skyline. Here and there we could see large lakers steaming along, leaving columns of smoke to drift off into the misty haze.

This is the largest freshwater lake in the world. It is 602 feet above sea level, 383 miles long and 160 miles wide. The area is 31,800 square miles, a little larger than the state of South Carolina. It has a depth of 1333 feet and its basin seems to be hewn out of solid rock. That is why the water is so clear, cold and pure that people drink it with safety. No weeds are seen around its shores. Most of its shoreline is bounded by these steep cliffs. This is especially true of its north shoreline. Cliffs rise there several hundred feet from the waters edge. Oh! this is a great world and Michigan has some wonderful scenery!

One big whispering pine tree stood right on the edge of the path leading to Miner's Castle as if it just loved the place where it grew and was determined to cling there against the erosion of wind and rain that threatened to uproot it. I picked some of the long, soft, glistening needles, they were beautiful.

While I was sitting in the sunshine, enjoying the solitude and grandeur of the panoramic view through my field glasses, Victor took my picture. All the pictures I have been describing are in my scrapbook. We climbed to the top of the rocks and clutching cautiously peered over at the dashing green water below. It looked green against the yellow sandstone bottom. The boys wanted their pictures taken on the rock, too, so we let them set there while we stood guard below. We would loved to have spent hours in this beautiful place but finally had to go back to the little clearing. We found that most of the tourists had left and several little striped chipmunks were whisking about, probably looking for crumbs. The boys had a great time watching them. They seemed very tame and would sit and look with their little black, shining eyes until you could almost touch them, then they would dart away in a flash.

We reached our tent about dark and after a good warm meal we were ready for bed and dreams of the places we had seen that day. Truly, this is the "Naples of America."

Next morning we were ready to leave, but happened to think that we hadn't visited the paper mills. We had seen the great piles of wood in the yard and had watched the men sawing lumber from big logs the day before, so we stopped and a guide showed us through the mill. It was very, very interesting. We saw the process of paper making from the time the bolts, bark and all were thrown into long chutes, ground into pulp, cooked in huge vats, rolled into sheets, finished, cut and ready for shipment. We spent about two hours here and I was presented with a lovely box of stationery, a souvenir that they gave every lady tourist.

Now we were ready for the long stretch, for we wanted to reach Fort Wilkins, as far north as we could get way up through the copper country, before nightfall.

On our way west of Munising we visited the falls in the Au Train River and it was the most beautiful one of all. The cold, sparkling waters came singing, playing, dashing and foaming over ledges of rocks in quite a wide riverbed. On each side there were lovely trees and all along the road, one could drink right out of the rocks, the purest, coldest water in the United States. I waded to the center of the falls and had my picture taken there.

We reached the interesting city of Marquette a little after

noon, where the cool breezes from Lake Superior blow over the town from the west. We saw the prison overlooking the lake but did not take time to drive to it. (Houghtelling the convicted murderer of a Genesee County child was there.) We went a few miles out to the State Park near Marquette. It was quite high above the town and was full of large, beautiful pine trees. We ate our lunch — canned salmon, bread, butter, fruit and I made tea. We met an older couple who had traveled all over. They had a good traveling outfit. On the way out, I saw a girl I had met in Mt. Pleasant, waved, but she didn't see me. It's a small world after all.

On our way we could see the dim outline of the Sugar Loaf Mountains toward the north, passed through Ishpeming and Negaunee, the center of the iron mining industry where the first discovery of iron ore in Michigan was made. We saw many glacial rocks and interesting lakes on the way. One little lake we passed was the prettiest one I have ever seen. It was perfectly round, as smooth as a mirror and fringed all around with little evergreens that were reflected in its surface. It reminded me of a fairy's looking glass. We saw many shimmering lakes in their setting of green clad rolling hills all along our whole journey.

I forgot to mention that at Marquette one enters the region of the ancient and complex rocks that are peculiar to the western and northern half of the Upper Peninsula. The farther north the rockier the land seemed.

There were many interesting names of rivers and creeks we passed, such as Pilgrim River, Plumbago Creek, Sturgeon Slough, Slapneck Creek, Anne Creek and Nett River. We passed a little town called Nathan.

We reached Keweenaw Bay quite late in the afternoon. Beautiful Baraga State Park is located right at the bend of the bay and it was full of tourist tents. Across the bay, lying in full view in the sunshine, is the city of L'Anse and it looked very nice that afternoon with its different colored buildings gleaming among the trees. Baraga is in full view of the people of L'Anse, in fact these cities are directly opposite each other across the bend in Keweenaw Bay. We did not stop in the park, but bought some bread (which we left lying on the car and lost), some cookies and kept traveling north on M 41. Isle Royal lies way out in

Keweenaw Bay. It is 55 miles from Keweenaw Peninsula and is considered one of the great natural parks of this universe. It has wild scenery, rocky hills, ridges, lakes, streams and an abundance of moose on its timbered slopes.

We were now entering the copper bearing district. The Copper Range, which extends clear through to the Porcupine Mountains in the northwest is the highest point in Michigan. This broad copper ridge, with bold bluffs, several hundred feet high is cut completely through by a remarkable gash 600 feet deep, occupied by Portage Lake which separates the twin cities of Houghton and Hancock. Here was the most interesting and beautiful scenery! On our way out of Hancock we climbed a HIGH hill and then parked to take in all the sights before going on. The two cities were lying below, separated by a long bridge over which traffic was creeping. We were so high! Many little lakes gleamed blue in the rolling, rocky hills and some were lost to view in the distance as they mingled with purple haze. One could see for miles and miles. Some smoky spot probably marked the site of a distant city.

Mine shafts dotted the landscape, many of them idle now because the decline in price of ore. However, many mines were in full operation. They are among the deepest in the world, tunneling under the cities and countryside, 4000 and 8000 feet deep. This ore, found here, is unique in that it is native copper. It is the metal itself, rather than some mineral compound. We did not have time to visit a mine that day as it was getting late in the afternoon, but on our way back we visited old Quincy Mine, looked down the long black shaft and in the large building saw the largest hoisting machine in the world in full operation, letting out its miles of long steel cables and bringing up cars filled with ore. We saw two men, their little lights on their caps gleaming, step in a car and were lowered deep into the dark, black hole. I would not want to be a miner but some people like it. The boys were so interested! The miners said, "Come on boys, want to go down?" Then they laughed and waved good-bye. We watched the lights flicker for a long time, far below. We brought home several pieces of native copper ore.

We passed through many mining towns that were full of

empty houses which were vacated when the ore played out and the mine closed.

Calumet was a busy place but we did not stop. We passed unique little villages, such as Mohawk, where there were few conveniences, at least in the part we saw.

We traveled on and on until darkness overtook us, uphill and down, around curves and through forests. It seemed as if we never would reach our destination. Finally, the welcome sign of "Michigan State Park" loomed up in the glare of our headlights. We followed the pointing hand and came to a store and tourist rest in a place called Copper Harbor. The place is only operated during the summer but deserted in winter because of heavy snow. Train and mail services cease. Probably a caretaker puts in a good winter's supply of food and fuel if anyone stays there at all.

We inquired about the tourist park and went on, only to lose our way. We had to go back and finally got the directions down pat.

We passed the Indian stockade of old Fort Wilkins, built by the English in the early nineteenth century, saw the gleaming tents in the darkness and knew that at last we had reached the right place. We were tired and the boys were all fast asleep! Fanny Hoe Lake lies within the fort and most of the tents were there, but we drove around a bit and found a level spot on the shore of Lake Superior. It was hard and stony but we threw and brushed the stones away from a space big enough for the tent, put it up, made the beds, ate a little bite and rolled in. We were beat.

Next morning we were awakened by the pounding of the surf near our tent and found that we were only a few feet from shore. The old lighthouse keeper told us that a storm would have washed into our tent. At one corner of the tent was a cluster of five pretty little birches and nearby some pines afforded us plenty of shade. It was an exquisite location. The shore was covered with beautiful, little stones of all colors and the blue water was gently lapping over them.

We were situated in a little bay and across to our right a point of land projected out into the water and at the end of this point was a little white lighthouse where the light flashed day and night to warn the many ships that passed. To our left another lighthouse had its beacon on at night and during periods of fog or mist. The lighthouse keeper lived there and kept a neat small home and yard. We went over and talked with him, watching as he lit the big lamp, one evening. He said boats got their bearings by lining up with the two lights across from each other. He said that whenever a ship went down in Lake Superior, it went down into cold storage and was rarely seen again. We stayed at this camp two days and were reluctant to leave. The boys loved it there, playing in the stones. "Bitty" wore his bathing suit a lot but didn't venture in much because the water was so cold.

The boys made a little fire on the shore among the stones and we roasted marshmallows one evening. The lighthouse beacon was flashing! flashing! and now and then a freighter would pass with lights from one end to the other. It was a very pretty sight. The moon, big, round and beautiful rose out of a frame formed by a fringe of evergreens.

We also visited the old fort and went through many of the old buildings that were built back in 1844. Names of a few of the British Garrison were carved on the walls in the old barracks. The brick fireplaces were very interesting.

The second day we pulled up camp and left grudgingly. We would liked to have stayed several days. Our closest tent neighbors had been there several weeks. They were from Owosso. This was our turnaround.

We started on our way homeward in the lovely afternoon sunshine and sure enjoyed the pretty drive over hills and through woods having missed it in the dark when we came.

We stopped at Eagle River and bought some postcards in the neat hotel office. It is a very small town. We saw an old school building that had been painted white and well preserved, with an iron fence built around the yard. A bronze plaque on the outside said that Justus Henry Rathbone, a school teacher there from 1858–59, wrote the ritual of the Knights of Pythias in that building.

We also visited Eagle Harbor and picked up unique stones from the shore. There's a place there where many agates are found but we didn't have time to stay long. We saw an imposing monument here, to Dr. Douglas Houghton, the first State Geologist of Michigan. Dr. Houghton, while on a geological exploration near Eagle Harbor in an Indian canoe, was caught by a storm and drowned with his Indian aide in Lake Superior. I took pictures here, then we hurried on.

Reaching Hancock about 4 P.M. we called on Dell's Grandma Opie. She was such a nice bright old lady. We enjoyed our visit, then drove down the hill and called on Rude's Mother, Mrs. Fien. She was very surprised to see us. They have a nice neat home. A large hill lies back of it defaced with mine shafts.

We ate our lunch in the tourist park at Houghton on the banks of Portage Lake, then hastened on our way. We drove until dark, south on US 141 through a long stretch of sparsely settled land until we reached Crystal Falls. A man directed us to Bewabic Park, a pay camp, and it was the neatest camp we had found. There were several deer fenced in at Bewabic Park. The boys enjoyed petting and feeding them. Tall stately trees, hydrants, conveniently located, lovely green grass and neatly painted tables and benches made it very attractive. There were swings and slides for the children and beautiful Fortune Lake, with its shining water and good fishing, boating and bathing facilities were right in the camp. We met people here from Howard City whose little girl took music lessons from Marjorie Carothers. We hated to leave the next morning but had to be on our way again as soon as we could pack up and take some more pictures. We took pictures of a big pine log that had 1156 board feet of lumber. It was donated to Bewabic Park by Herman and William Holmes.

We passed through some more iron mining country at Iron Mountain, Norway and Vulcan, visited a mine and found some fool's gold, and sparkling chunks of ore formations. We loaded our car right down. We passed through a little part of Wisconsin on our way at Spread Eagle and crossed a tributary of the Brule River, famous for its visits from Calvin Coolidge. Also, crossed the Menominee River.

We passed through Escanaba, Gladstone and around beautiful Little Bay DeNoc, a part of Lake Michigan, out US 2, past Big Bay DeNoc and toward Manistique. A sign pointed north from the main highway toward the big Indian Spring, so we took this road about five miles in. This "Big Spring" on the west side of Indian Lake is a wonder point. It boils up through rock fissures at the bottom of a pool 100 x 200 feet and nearly 50 feet deep. The water is crystal clear and icy cold. We rode on a little raft out to the middle of it and watched pennies zig-zag to the bottom. We all had a drink of the clear water that never ceases bubbling. This spring feeds Indian Lake. I bought some souvenirs of "Spring Ketch-ita-keepie" as they sometimes call it. The road to and from the spring was very rough, but we were glad we went to see it.

We passed through the nice city of Manistique and on east until darkness overtook us. We found no state park, so inquired as to a camping place and a man directed us to Gulliver's Lake where he said some people were camping and it was the only place he knew about so we followed his directions. It was about a mile back in a dark woods on a bad road. We found the campers alright and they started helping to put up our tent, almost breaking it and the beds too, but as soon as our lantern was lit my! oh, my! the millers came by the millions. I tried to fry some hamburg and finally succeeded but had to keep it covered. Finally, we brushed each other off and darted into the tent one by one, closing the flap quickly behind us. We succeeded in evading most of the insects but a few got inside and one or two into our food but we were too hungry to notice. A lady there said she thought she heard a bear prowling around the night before, so all in all our stay at Gulliver's Lake was none too pleasant and we were glad to leave early as possible the next morning.

We traveled east to Garnet, then north to M-28 and east again. I drove much of the way through a rather desolate region where we did not pass a car sometimes for miles. It was a bright beautiful afternoon and we reached Sault Ste. Marie about 3 P.M. We wanted to buy some fish so went straight to the fish market on the waters edge and caught them just before they closed the place for the day. We bought a big, fresh lake trout that had been caught that morning, ten miles out in Lake Superior. The man told us it weighed about four pounds. The boys wanted to take turns carrying it in the car, until I feared they would wear it out.

We then hurried to visit the locks and never having seen them before, found them very interesting. We watched several boats lock down and then visited the power plant. We had to hurry so we nosed toward St. Ignace and just in time to catch the ferry. The Sault is a pretty place with nice parks and trees and we would liked to have stayed longer. I forgot to mention that we almost decided to ferry across the St. Mary's River from the Sault into Canada and home that way. We boarded the ferry, but when we found out how far it was and how much it would cost we knew we were in wrong. The inspector told us to just turn our car around on the Canadian side and drive right back on again. We did and were glad we decided to go home via Mackinaw City.

As I mentioned above, we reached St. Ignace and the ferry just in time. We were getting very hungry and my mind was on the big fish the boys were holding, but we did get out of the car and on deck to watch the people promenade. Several girls, who thought they were smart, were smoking cigarettes and some were playing cards. They made us disgusted so we spent most of our time watching the water, which was much more inspiring. When we left the ferry we were much amused watching a poor, nervous woman try to drive her car off. She looked this way and that, knocked her hat off in her excitement and finally four or five men said, "Come on boys, roll her out of here" and so they pushed her out. Just as we got in line to disembark we found we had a flat tire so had to stay on the dock until it was fixed. I thought of my poor old fish that the sleepy boys had been carrying part of the way on their laps.

We got to the state camp in Mackinaw City about 10 P.M. and it was full to overflowing for it was Saturday night. We found about the only remaining spot for a tent right by the drive, so Victor started putting up the tent and I helped him fix the beds. The boys were asleep, so I got "Mr. Fish", put some papers on the ground and proceeded to clean him. Then I went down to the tables and stoves in the big community kitchen and found the fires about out, but scouted around and located a little wood, put my fish on, cooked potatoes, made some coffee and opened a can of peas. Then I roused the boys with much difficulty, (although Robert was wide awake as soon as he knew there was something to eat) took them down to the tables, fed them and then Victor put them back to bed. I was eating all this time by my lonesome, (except now and then a person or two would pass and look amused), when lo! the lights were turned out, for it was twelve o'clock. I was in total darkness but never stopped eating as long as I could find the aperture in my face. I never lost a mouthful. Finally, Victor came with our lantern and I cleared the things

OLD TOWNSHIP HALL BURNS

I always kept my camera "on the ready." Once in a while you get a shot at such an event. The photograph was taken on my way home from Coleman.

OUR FISHERMAN

Son Robert caught a green bass from Little Traverse Lake, August 29, 1934.

away and washed dishes before I retired, a very, very tired person, but not hungry.

We arose quite early next morning, made coffee and ate the rest of the cooked fish, then started out for home after inspecting beautiful Mackinaw State Park. I would like to camp there a whole week.

We came around by Higgins Lake and past the Forest Reserve near Harrison where I saw a rattler coiled beside the road near a swampy woods. It had black diamond-like patches on its back. I wanted to stop and finish him off but Victor wouldn't stop. Chicken.

We reached Mt. Pleasant about 3 P.M. and stopped and ate lunch, then on to St. Louis where we stayed all night with Sister Mid and Uly. We were glad to reach here for our money had ran out and we had to borrow two dollars from Uly for gas.

We came home next day, a tired but happy bunch of people, having taken in more worthwhile sights than most people would think of taking in on an eleven day vacation trip.

CHAPTER XI

BEST YEARS OF OUR LIVES

IN 1933 OUR parents celebrated their fiftieth wedding anniversary and my sisters and I and our families planned and hosted a dinner and program for them. It was held in the old IMA Auditorium in downtown Flint. All of our family and friends helped them celebrate this festive event.

My mother had been in failing health for some time, so my sister, Grace, came to care for her. In 1936 at age 78 Ma passed away. She had requested that my sisters and I sing at her funeral. I didn't know if I would be able to do it, but I prayed for God to give me the strength without breaking down. My prayers were answered and we sang "The Last Mile of the Way" for my mother with dry eyes and strong voices.

After Ma's death, my sister, Mildred, and her son, Jack, came to live with Pa on Indiana Avenue. She had been divorced and was teaching school. Living so close to us, Jack spent a lot of time at our house on Broadway and was just like one of our own family. He and our three boys would have a lot of fun together. One time, when Jack was staying overnight, they had a pillow fight and there were feathers everywhere!

We were a happy family, and it seemed there never was a dull moment. The boys were in Central High School now and

A GREAT CELEBRATION

A great celebration for my parents on their Golden Wedding Day was held at the I.M.A. Auditorium in Flint. They never had it easy. My father was in turn, a farmer, share cropper, lumber jack and minister. My mother was a devoted wife and mother. They were fine Christian people and we have always been proud of them and what they have done for us, their five girls.

PA'S ONLY REDHEAD

After Mother died, Pa's hair turned white on top. He was a great father.

FLINT CENTRAL HIGH SCHOOL CONCERT BAND

My boys all held first chairs in their respective sections of this band. Vernon on clarinet, Robert on bass and Victor Jr. on French horn during their high school years in Flint, Michigan.

played in the high school band. Practice time was deafening, with the blasts of Bob's trumpet, the toots and squeals of Vernon's clarinet and then there were the soft notes of Bid's French horn. They all wound up in first chair of their sections.

I had always wanted my boys to learn to appreciate music and encouraged each of them to play a musical instrument. My wishes were carried out, sometimes reluctantly, into their high school years, until the call of sports took over their interest; Vernon with basketball, Robert into track and Victor, Jr. into football.

Bob loved pets and teased until we got him a pair of bunnies. All went well for a time. Despite his care, he went to feed them one morning and came to the house crying, with two dead bunnies in his hand. He was so heartbroken! Later, he brought a German Shepherd dog home. It was a beautiful, young dog but had no collar or any mark of identification on it. We said, "No dog!" With a few tears and a few begs, we told him he could keep her overnight, then in the morning try and find her owner. That was the beginning of a twelve year life with Queenie.

The boys had lots of friends. One morning I was trying to get breakfast when there were seven boys in the kitchen. As I look back now, it seems those were the best years of our lives.

About this time (I think 1939) I went out to get the milk on the back step, fell and broke my left arm. We lived next to the fire station and the firemen heard me and came to help. They called the doctor and when he came to the house he knew I would have to go to the hospital. Meanwhile, he put a brace on to hold it in place. I was in such pain I could hardly bear it. I told Victor to please help me. He got down on his knees and prayed. Immediately I felt my arm shift slightly and the pain was relieved. When we arrived at Hurley Hospital and the doctor x-rayed my arm, it was set perfectly so they only had to put a cast on. This is just another example of the power of Jesus to heal.

VERNON IN BAND UNIFORM

Our boys preferred the Marching Band where they could strut their stuff.

BAND WAITING FOR THE TRAIN

The band at ease in formation on the tracks of the Michigan Central in front of the Downtown Depot at the River. Alf Landon, Presidential candidate, is coming by train to Flint, 1936.

MARCHING ON SAGINAW STREET

This band was inspirational for all three boys and became, for several years an important part of our family life. Robert is here in the middle of the formation with his bass horn.

EVERYBODY LOVES A PARADE

A photo of the west side of Saginaw Street looking north from 3rd Street soon after the streetcar tracks were lifted. Flint was a fine, safe town, in 1939.

QUEENIE AND "TINEE"

It was a humanitarian act. Queenie was only to stay overnite, but she stayed for twelve years. She could almost talk to me.

HER SEVEN PUPS

Dogs and boys have a lot in common at this age. Victor and I decided not to deny them this experience. L to R: Robert, Victor Jr. and Buddy Rutter, our next door neighbor.

THE GROCERY STORE

The store opened in the fall of 1924 at 1918 Minnesota Ave. Victor also held a position at Buick Division, so you know who was his slave.

MR. RIESE'S CAR

Mr. Riese's car was decapitated and nearly took Waso's Station along for the ride. He was hardly scratched.

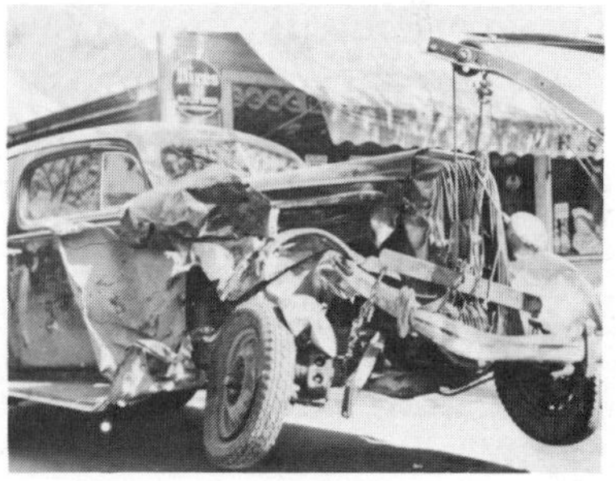

MY HELPLESS
NEW CHEVROLET

My helpless new Chevy was a mess. Everybody in my car was hurt. I was sore for a month. The Chevrolet never recovered.

Crash Injuries Four on North Dixie

"FLINT, Jan. 24 — Four persons were injured in a two-car crash at the north Dixie Highway and Stanley Road, sheriff's deputies reported today. In the city, injury accidents were unreported but investigators said property damage crashes were high because of the slippery streets."

Those injured in the county accident were:

THEODORE ALLEN RIESE, 30, of Detroit.

MRS. JUSTINA E. SMITH, of 1702 Broadway, Flint.

MARY CAROTHERS, 22, of 1314 Walker Street, Flint.

HARRY McCANN, 25, of 1314 Walker Street, Flint.

Witnesses said the automobiles driven by Riese and Mrs. Smith crashed head-on. The accident apparently was caused by the slippery pavement, deputies said. The injured were taken to Hurley Hospital where attendants reported their condition as good. Miss Carothers and Mrs. Smith suffered possible fractures of the ankle. McCann was treated for cuts and bruises while the Detroiter was treated for minor face injuries. It was lucky no one was killed.

A heavy snow which blanketed Flint Streets last night moved traffic today at a slow pace. City DPW employees coated the more dangerous intersections with sand.

This happened during the pre-salt days.

When we moved to Flint, Victor started working for Buick. After we moved to Broadway, in addition to his job at Buick, we started a grocery in the garage at the back of our lot. It was nice, but soon became a work place for me as well. We had a phone from the house to the garage and sometimes as I was busy washing or getting a meal, Victor would call and say, "Come give me a lift." We soon took orders and delivered groceries in a small pickup truck. With three active boys on my hands I had a load, so we hired a girl to help. We often used anything that could not be sold, such as fruit that had soft spots etc. One day when the store was full of customers, our hired girl popped her head in the front door and yelled, "Have you got anything rotten for supper?"

So it went until war clouds gathered. The store prospered and we hired a young man to help. When rationing came we

A GOING BUSINESS

Having been reared in the Smiths Brothers Grocery in Stanton, Victor knew how to make it go — with help.

SUNDAY SCHOOL SUPERINTENDENT

This was taken June 3, 1940 in the Sanctuary of the First Pilgrim Holiness Church of Flint.

BUICK FACTORY TRANSPORTATION ENTRANCE

This is where Victor worked. I snapped his picture from the gate in the doorway with a shiny new Buick in the foreground.

NEW BUICK POWER PLANT

The photograph was taken from Leith Street looking down Buick Division Street.

ASBURY M.E. CHURCH CONSTRUCTION

It was most interesting to watch this teamster direct this beautiful span of mules with a gentle gee and haw across the street from our store. He hardly put any pressure on the reins. The shovel was a steam powered coal burner.

began to lose business. In the meantime, I had the thought that I wanted to teach again someday, when the boys were older. I had a Sunday School class of women that I enjoyed and took a three year correspondence course from Owosso Bible College. I also studied a year of Greek from Rev. Scott of Flint, to learn more about the Bible. Then I helped with Vacation Bible School each summer and the Christmas program, too, which I loved.

Then came World War II and our form of living was changed completely. I was glad that I had gone to three terms of summer school at Mt. Pleasant during those busy years, for I wasn't sure now what the future would bring.

CHAPTER XII

WORLD WAR II

OUR THREE BOYS were out of Central High School and Vernon, twenty one, was already married and had a baby boy. All three boys wanted to enlist. We had decisions to make.

The first to go was Robert, who entered the Air Corps. Then Victor Jr, eighteen, joined the Marines. They left for training in California and when they went it was heartbreaking. The house seemed so empty. For a time we maintained the store, but business kept going down, so I got a job at Buick for a time to keep my mind occupied. Finally, Vernon enlisted in the Air Force, too, and went to Mississippi and Georgia for training, where he got his wings. Days dragged on and we finally came to a decision. We sold out everything in the store, rented our house furnished to a nice couple and went to California to be near our boys, for we knew they would be going across when their training was completed.

We had no automobile, so the trip west was by train and we enjoyed the mountains in Colorado. The scenery was lovely all the way. We crossed the Great Divide, then turned southwest across wasteland where there were no signs of human habitation, nothing but sagebrush and Joshua Trees. We were heading toward Los Angeles. At night we were told to keep our shades drawn so no light would show. We were nearing the Pacific, our enemies were watching, so had to be on the alert. Our luggage consisted of two small trunks and several bundles which were left in the baggage room while we found a hotel not far from the station where we would spend the night. We walked to the hotel and in the morning I learned we had walked down Skid Row, one of the toughest streets in L.A.! After we got settled in our room, I went out to take a look at the pretty neon signs, and a drunk man tottered toward me. That was enough — I hurried back to my room.

We knew Robert was at LaMoor Air Base in northern California, so next morning we bought tickets and had our baggage checked to LaMoor. Our seats on the train were numbered and I had the tickets. Our train was called and I went to the gate to board it, but Victor was nowhere to be found. I had him paged several times, but no Victor. At last I had to go without him, up the long ramp to the train that was scheduled to leave on time. I was desperate! What should I do? A station attendant in a gray uniform was passing as the train started and I reached out with Victor's ticket and called, "Give this to Victor Smith!" The train went on for a few miles to Glendale. I felt tears welling up. The train started to move slowly. As I looked up, there was Victor coming in the door. The station attendant had seen him running to the train, gave him the ticket and hurried him to a taxi that caught the train in Glendale, just as it was moving out. I just cried with joy — too happy to scold him. He had been looking for our bundles, but they were already aboard the train. We went to the diner and had a delicious breakfast. It was a lovely day and the scenery was beautiful. We rounded curves and went through a tunnel where the train made a big loop and came out at a lower level. It is called the Hocapa Loop. From the window I could see the engine up ahead puffing smoke and the rear coach at the other side of the loop.

At the base we found that Robert was out on the training field. An officer sent word for him and gave him the rest of the day off. We ran to meet him. He looked so sweet in his cadet uniform with his hat tipped jauntily on the side of his head. He looked happy and was smiling, so we knew he liked his training. We had dinner that night with Robert at the base and were treated royally.

The next day, we returned to Los Angeles, for Victor had to find a job. We had to re-check our baggage, and when we got back to look for it, a trunk was missing. It just could not be found, so they let me go into the baggage room where there were dozens of trunks and suitcases. I looked, but no trunk. I was about to give up when I spied one all by itself in a corner. It was mine, but the tag had been lost off. I had to identify the contents before they would open it. It WAS mine.

At Los Angeles we found there was plenty of work in the aviation plants. They were putting out planes by the hundreds. We heard that North American Aviation, in the little town of Inglewood, a few miles from L.A., would be a good place to apply. We went there and both got a job. I wanted to be a riveter, but was checked in as an assembler and glad afterward, for riveting was much harder. Victor checked in the section where heavier parts of the planes were assembled.

We found a nice apartment at Manhattan Beach, a few miles from the North American Aviation plant, right on the ocean, high up on Highland Avenue where we had a good view of the beautiful Pacific. We loved the roar of the ocean at night. We soon found friends we could ride to work with, for we still had no car. We were put on the night shift. The plant was entirely covered with chicken wire and so disguised that it looked like ordinary landscape from the air. It even had brush and trees.

I liked my job from the start. I had to learn how to use an electric drill and at first broke so many drills (40) that I was afraid to go to the window and ask for more. But I soon got so efficient I hardly ever broke one. I assembled the parts that were used in the wings of the Mustang fighter planes for gun turrets. It had to be accurate and I realized I could be responsible for a fighter pilot's life if I didn't do a job right.

We worked hard and were anxious for the time to come when we could visit Victor, Jr. We always called him Bitty when a baby—he was so tiny—and it finally ended up Bid. We had visited Robert, now it was Bid's turn for us to visit him at the San Diego Marine Base. That day came at last and we met him one morning. What a happy, but tearful, reunion! He had been so homesick, but was soon cheerful and happy to have dinner with us. He also brought a buddy along, another homesick kid from

**PATRIOTIC AIRCRAFT
FACTORY WORKERS**

*I worked on Mustang P-51
Fighters and B-25 Medium
Bomber assembly. Victor
was in crating and ship-
ping. This was the least we
could do as two of our boys
became pilots and the third
a parachute rigger.*

Flint. We had fun that day. We made a few other visits, but time
was precious and we had to stick close to our duties.

One day Robert met us at a little town called Visalia, half-
way from LaMoor base. We had lunch in a nice little cafe there.
A radio was playing a new tune I had never heard before. It was
"White Christmas" and Bing Crosby was singing, "I'm Dreaming
of a White Christmas." We kissed Robert good-bye, realizing we
might never see him again. To this day, when I hear "White
Christmas", tears come to my eyes. It brings back the memory of
that day.

Time went on and we began getting letters from the boys'
girl friends. They wanted to come out and see them. We also got
word that the boys were being transferred to new bases; Bid to
the Marine base in the Mojave Desert in northern California and
Robert to the Air Force base at Douglas, Arizona, right on the
Mexican border.

A letter came from Robert saying that Beth was on her way
and to please meet her at the train in L.A. I took the day off to

VICTOR Jr. (BID) IN TRAINER PLANE

He was at Mojave Marine Base and liked all of it. I could not get as excited about it as any of our boys could. Danger lurked everywhere.

meet the train, which was an hour late. It finally arrived with a large crowd of passengers coming down the ramp. I strained my eyes to find her and there she was, coming down the ramp with a little plaid cap perched jauntily over her curls, and she was smiling, so happy to be near us. We stayed all night in a hotel room because it was getting late. We were so tired that we did not awake the next morning until nearly noon, so did not arrive at our apartment in Manhattan Beach until in the afternoon. Robert visited us and they decided they wanted to get married before he went across. He was a Second Lieutenant and would be getting his wings. We went shopping for a wedding dress and finally found one. It was not just what she wanted, but it was pale yellow and of soft material that looked lovely on her. It was street length and nice for any occasion.

The day was set for the wedding at Douglas, Arizona on March 9, 1943. They were married in the chapel of a Methodist Church by the pastor. Robert had earned his wings and was dressed in his best Air Force uniform. His Air Force flight instructor and his wife were their attendants. It was a beautiful, but solemn occasion. After a nice wedding dinner we kissed the happy newlyweds good-bye and went back to our work at North American Aviation. A few days later another letter arrived from Bid. Helen was on her way, and we knew they probably wanted to be married, too, but they were so young. Could we decide to let them?

Finally the day arrived for Helen's arrival at the big railway station in L.A. She too looked happy and smiling, but burst into tears when she met Bid looking so nice in his Marine uniform. She had been so brave to travel all alone and this was such a joyful reunion! We could see it would be just no use to stop this wedding, so plans were made and when the day arrived, we went to a small town not far from the Marine base in the desert where they were married in April of 1943. They were married by a Nazarene pastor in his church parsonage. His wife sang "Blest Be The Tie That Binds." It was really a nice wedding and Helen looked so sweet. There was no church dinner, but I had brought a wedding cake and a delicious lunch for the four of us. We went way out in the desert and found a spot where we could eat. I took a picture of the happy couple sitting on the sandy desert floor, ready to cut their wedding cake.

They found a nice little apartment right at the Marine base and we went back to our work again at North American Aviation. We knew the boys would be going across soon, so we left them there and made plans to leave for home in Flint.

Meanwhile, we had been getting letters from Vernon and Mary. She and little Gary had gone to Valdosta, Georgia Air Base to be with Vernon for awhile. He had learned to fly the big transport planes called boxcars. Now he, too, was a Second Lieutenant and would soon be getting his wings. When we got that word we hurried to leave. We planned a longer trip home, so we could see more of the country while we had the chance.

We bought tickets and checked our baggage, to go by way of the Great Northern Railroad to Oregon and down through the central states. We had seats assigned to us in a nice coach that could be converted into a sleeper at night. We had six or seven bundles packed in the rack overhead. One was a big hatbox packed with oranges and a few other things I had tucked in at the last moment.

Spring was well on the way and the day was beautiful when we left. It took some time to get to the suburbs of the great city of Los Angeles. We were soon headed northward along the beautiful Pacific. Now and then we caught a glimpse of its blue water. After a time the high banks obscured its view and we could see mountains ahead. The train was nearing the Cascade Mountains. They were a lovely sight, with sparkling waterfalls rushing down all the way, for miles. Between the falls dogwood was in bloom, down the slopes, intermingled with a purple flowering bush that added color to the scene. It was a lovely sight and Victor always let me sit by the window. He would take a nap now and then, but I didn't want to miss anything. Toward night we had to pull our shades down and that was my duty. How I hated to shut the view off before sunset. The conductor ordered "shades drawn." The Japs might see a patch of light. As he passed down the coach I sneaked a peek under the shade. He turned, pointed his finger at me and said sternly, "Pull that shade down!" That was the last time I tried that.

The city of Portland, Oregon was the next place of interest. It is beautifully situated in a climate where the air is fresh and free from smog.

The second day began to get tiresome. We walked the coach for exercise. We ate in the diner now and then, but nibbled on our lunch I had made, to save money.

We crossed the Great Divide where water trickles toward the Pacific on one side and toward the Atlantic on the other. The train left off coaches at a few stops and we had to change to another coach. That was quite a job with all the bundles we had.

VERNON IN TRAINING

At Hawthorne Field, Orangebury, South Caroline with PT-17 Stearman trainer plane in background. Vernon is on the extreme right with the squad instructor in the center.

DAD, MOTHER AND MARINE BID

Proud as we could be of our Marine, we were in San Diego, California, on Christmas Day, 1942.

ROBERT SAYING
GOOD-BYE TO ME

In the park at Visalia, California on the Saturday following Thanksgiving in 1942. I felt close to all my boys and especially so during these trying days of war.

After two or three trips we had everything moved except the hat box. When I went back, it was gone! The train had stopped at Bonners Ferry, Idaho and we were several miles on our way. I got in contact with the conductor and he telegraphed back to Bonners Ferry. The hatbox had been put off when passengers unloaded. "Never mind," the conductor said, "give me your address. The Great Northern Railroad will see that you get your box." A few days after we arrived in Flint, the box was brought to our door. Not one article was missing or one orange spoiled.

It had taken us five days on the train, changing trains at Chicago. We were completely tired out. The couple who rented our house did not want to move, so we went to live in Vernon and Mary's place and that made them happy, as Mary wanted to be near Vernon. We soon left to be with him at Valdosta, Georgia the day he got his wings. He was a Second Lieutenant now. We were proud of him as he stood his 6'3" tall while Mary pinned his wings on his lapel.

Letters came from the children out west. We had left them with our blessing and they were very happy.

Bob was sent to Florida for further training and to await orders for overseas. Beth returned to Flint. We were very comfortable in Vernon's little house at 2220 Hoff Street. I put our three star flag in the window and joined the Homedale Blue Star Mothers Club Auxiliary to do all I could to help the war effort. I got a job at Marvel Carburetor where small parts were made for war planes. My job was inspecting. It was monotonous, but each piece had to be absolutely accurate.

Time dragged slowly on as we awaited word of the boys last trips home before going overseas. It came from Robert first. He could be with us for only a short time. It was another sad farewell, but we had to be brave. He left soon after for overseas duty in England. He was assigned to a B26 bomber with a crew of seven, a pilot, co-pilot, bombardier-navigator, crew chief and three gunners. His letters told of the preparation for going into action, but were brief for they were censored. Then it came — he had gone on a mission across the English Channel and all had returned safely. We wrote him to put an X (kiss) at the end of his letters for each mission, and soon letters came with several "kisses." To keep up every day, we prayed and watched the news to see how the war was going on all fronts. Our days were spent in anxious waiting for news and sometimes sleepless nights, but we carried on.

Robert had flown over 30 missions now and had returned safely each time. Sometimes his plane was hit and there were holes in it and once a piece of flak passed his face and could have killed him, but he was spared. The missions numbered in the 40's now, we believed. We knew he couldn't add so many X's now. We prayed day and night and sent cheerful letters and never complained about our worries, it would not help. We sent boxes of goodies, but no answer came. We kept on working. Then one day my daughter-in-law, Beth, received a Western Union telegram from the Secretary of War; Robert was "missing in action." No one except those who had gone through a similar experience could understand the anguish of that day. Had his plane crashed? Was he still alive? The news had come when we got home from work. Our supper was tasteless and we spent a sleepless night. It seemed our strength had gone, but we had to be brave. Days went by and no word came. We watched the papers. One day a battered box of fruit and cookies arrived with a clearly printed notice, "Missing in action." We knew it was close to D Day and this probably happened when the Air Force made their all-out effort to conquer. Two weeks went by and we grew weaker. At last the day came when I could bear it no longer; my strength was gone. Then the phone rang and it was Beth. She had word from friends in a western state that his plane was seen going down, but several parachutes were sighted. That gave us hope! Then news came that he was a prisoner of war of the German government. Not until the war was over and he returned, did we get the full story of how he crashed while flying his 60th mission over France near Chateau Thierry, when an engine was shot out of his plane.

Robert recalled from his diary and memory, after the war, the events leading up to that day. In March 1943, as a young (twenty-one year old) inexperienced pilot, fresh out of flying school, Class 43C, he was assigned as a co-pilot to the 387th bomb group, 557th squadron flying the B-26 twin engine medium bomber (Martin Marauder). During the early training stages, the B-26 Martin Marauder had a reputation for being a "hot" and very difficult airplane to handle, requiring special pilot skills. Derogatory names of "Widow Maker" and "Martin Murderer" came about as a result of the many accidents and pilots killed learning to fly this fast and maneuverable medium bomber. During the war, however, the B-26 eventually gained considerable recognition for its bombing accuracy and ability to take a lot of punishment and keep on flying.

The squadron left for overseas assignment to the European theater of operations (E.T.O.) in June, 1943. Refueling stops were made in Greenland and Iceland as they flew their own planes across the North Atlantic into Scotland and England.

From their English base, located approximately eighteen miles from London, they were sent into action against German installations and defenses mainly in the occupied countries of France, Belgium and Holland. Their first action was a bombing mission on August 15, 1943 against a German airfield (Fort Rouge Airdrome) at St. Omer, France. This first mission proved to be an eye opener for the inexperienced crew as they encountered heavy "flak" from German anti-aircraft defenses in delivering their bombs to the target. The seriousness of war was driven home as they counted the seventeen "flak" holes in their plane upon returning safely to their English base.

Many missions were to follow; some they labeled "milk runs"

NORTH ATLANTIC FLIGHT

In June 1943, planes were needed at English bases. Robert was co-pilot and is in the middle, first row, flanked on the left by the pilot and on the right by the bombardier-navigator. The second row (L to R) includes the radio man, crew chief and two gunners.

FIRST LT.
ROBERT N. SMITH

Robert with his parachute taken the day before being shot down, May 26, 1944, over Chartres, France. At the time, he was a veteran of 59 successful missions.

WORRY WART AND CREW

Back row, L to R: Lt. Young, Sgt. McDonald, our Robert and Sgt. Koluder. Front row, L to R: Sgt. Middleton, Sgt. Keim and a member of the ground crew. Robert flew 30 missions in this plane.

WORRY WART RETURNS

This plane flew 113 missions between 8/15/43 and 10/12/44. It crash-landed on base after being badly shot up. By looking closely you can make out our son's name as co-pilot under the window. No one was injured.

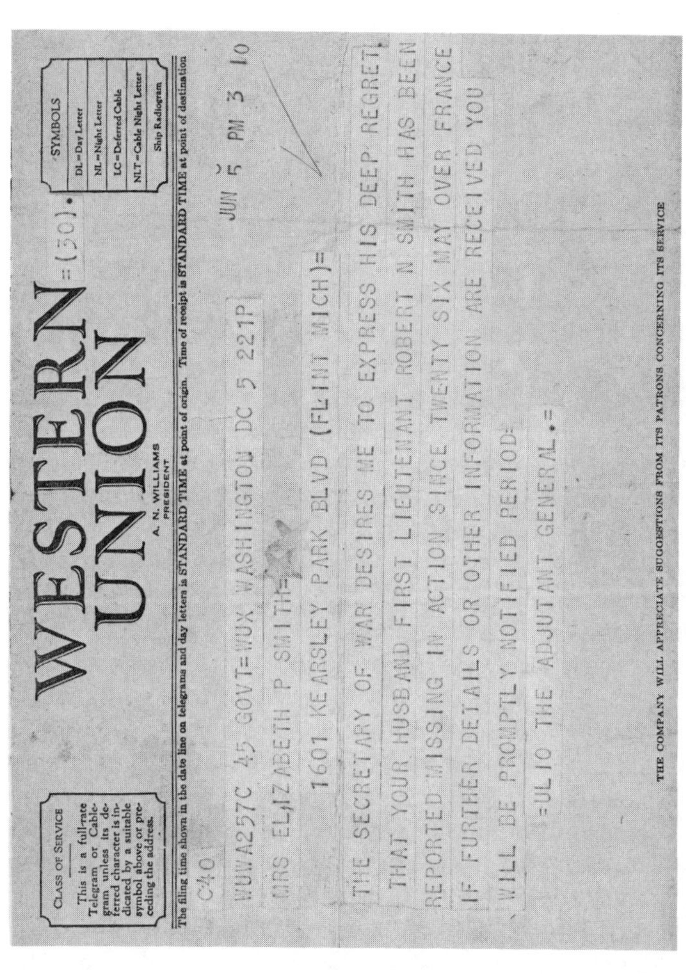

MISSING IN ACTION

This was not a pleasant message for a young wife to receive. It threw the whole family into shock.

because of the lack of German resistance, and others proved to be extremely hazardous with "flak" bursting on all sides. German fighters also attacked the formation on several occasions. Battle damage was encountered on many of these missions and other ships were seen going down. Some exploded and others went down in flames but Robert and crew had always returned safely.

On May 26, 1944 the 557th squadron was briefed to bomb a German fighter base located just outside Chartres, France, fifty miles northwest of Paris. This was Robert's 60th mission and he was looking forward to completion of his tour and going home. Having by this time gained considerable combat experience, he had been placed in command of a ship and crew. The mission objective was to destroy the base to reduce the increasing threat of German fighter attacks on allied bombing missions. A second, but important strategy was to coordinate the B-26 mission with the long-range four engine bomber raids (B-17 Flying Fortresses and B-24 Liberators). The B-26s were scheduled to go in ahead of the heavy's and "scramble" the German fighters into the air to run them out of gas. The long range bombers would then proceed in to bomb targets deep inside Germany, hopefully with disrupted and reduced fighter opposition.

The take-off and assembly of the 18 plane formation was without incident and the B-26 Marauders were soon crossing the English Channel and heading into German occupied France. When over enemy territory, evasive action was always used to disrupt the deadly aim of the experienced German anti-aircraft gun batteries below. Bomber pilots had a high degree of respect for the skill and accuracy of the German 88 MM gun crews and never flew in a straight line for over fifteen or twenty seconds. It was like a contest with the Germans always trying to guess which way they would turn next in order to lead and hit the formation flying at an altitude of 10,000 to 12,000 feet.

As they near the target area, the formation divides into three flights of six planes each and heads onto the bomb run. The German 88's, defending the target, find their range and open fire on the lead flight. Now on the bomb run, there is no turning aside and the flight tightens up and continues through the flak towards the target. As Robert recalled to me, just seconds before bomb release, a burst of flak is sighted ahead, a second one a little closer, a third just in front and the plane lurches with an explosion. The fourth one has found its mark. Suddenly, the other planes in the formation disappear from view — only blue sky ahead. The plane is out of control and heading up into a stall. The elevator control does not respond to bring the nose down. The elevator trim tab control on the side of the console finally responds and the plane is nosed over into a steep angle to prevent a stall and spin. A quick survey reveals the right engine is blown away and the windshield is smashed. There is a large hole in the fuselage, (radio compartment) just behind the bulkhead where co-pilot, 1st Lt. Neil Bartholomew, is sitting. No one in front appears injured. The plane doesn't appear to be on fire but the danger of exploding gas tanks and the bomb load is of great concern as Robert and Neil exchange concerned glances. While Neil slides his seat back to let the bombardier (2nd Lt. Walter Wright) crawl out of the nose, Robert turns to the left engine but something is wrong. A B-26 can fly on one engine and the left engine looks all right but the R.P.M. has dropped to around 1200–1300 instead of 2000 where it should be. Both the manual control and electrical feathering switch fail to bring it up. Full throttle on the engine brings no response, no surge of power. The plane is now losing altitude rapidly and vibrating badly. They are on what they refer to as "their way in". A crash is imminent! Robert pulls and hooks the emergency bomb release and salvoes the bomb load (two 2000 lb bombs). He sounds the alarm and calls on intercom for the crew to bail out. Bombardier Wright is the first to leave, going out through the open bombays located midway in the plane. Before co-pilot Neil leaves, he pulls Robert's flak suit off, an act that would considerably enhance Roberts escape from the plane. There is no communication now with the three gunners in back, over the intercom. (Staff Sgt. George Farfaras, Sgt. Clyde Morton, Sgt. William Brown). A vibrating airplane is difficult to control and maintain level with the trim tabs. With the right engine gone and the right wing and fuselage badly damaged, the drag on the right side was severe. This makes it difficult to keep it from rolling over. Robert knew that when he left the pilot compartment he would have to move fast to get out in time with no one at the controls. Not daring to remain at the controls much longer with his personal exit chances getting slimmer by the second, he made a final attempt to trim and steady the Marauder Attack Bomber. It was now descending rapidly at a steep angle. This B-26 with its short wings had a reputation when in A-1 condition for a steep decent and was often referred to as the flying brick.

Now believing and hoping all three gunners had cleared the plane from the rear escape hatches, he slid his seat back, unbuckled and made a break for the bombays. Entering the debris strewn radio compartment, there to his surprise, ahead on the bombay catwalk sits Neil waiting for him. As Robert comes through Neil goes out.

Centrifugal forces began to grip Robert's body and hamper his progress through the narrow bulkhead openings as he makes a beeline for his only exit from the wreck. His parachute harness usually caught on something in training but not this time. Luck was with him.

He dives into the bombay opening headlong and suddenly finds himself suspended in mid air and powerless to do anything about it. Robert had a helpless feeling as he struggled against the forces holding him within the body of the plane.

Then suddenly he drops free. The plane rolled to the right and away from him.

As Robert recalls, this plane wasn't through with him yet! Once free, his training and instinct told him to delay pulling the rip cord to allow falling as close to the ground as possible before opening the chute. He didn't want to be a floating target for the Germans in the area below. He told me that he remembers tumbling head over heels a couple times then going for the ground head first, picking up speed. He looked at the ground below for a sense of distance when suddenly he sees a plane coming. A quick mental observation warns him that he is dropping directly into the path of the oncoming plane. Fear grips him and he almost pulls the rip cord but at the last instant doesn't. The plane passes directly beneath him. As it goes by he gets a good look at it. The right engine is missing. Now he realizes this is his own plane he has just left. He recalls that he must have dropped directly into the path of his own plane as it rolled over and spiraled back around on its way down.

With that close call over, he tries to look again at the fast approaching ground searching for something recognizable. It feels like he has fallen a long way as he tries to focus his eyes through the rushing air. Through his blurred vision, a team of white horses suddenly come into view. With the sudden realization of what they are and the size of them, he yanks the rip cord from the harness. Having never experienced a parachute jump before, it was a shock to see the entire release wire come loose and strung out in front of his face like it had broken. Fear grips him again as he wonders if the chute will open.

Then suddenly he is jerked upright as the chute opens and billows above him.

Efforts to turn the chute around and land facing with the wind drift proved fruitless and he lands going backwards into a plowed field. The chute drags him on his back until he can struggle to his feet. He has landed in the same field with the team of white horses driven by a farmer who is plowing. The farmer barely seems to notice as Robert gets out of his parachute harness. He glances around for a place to hide but the freshly plowed field is big and open. His plane had crashed in the next field and is burning. Fifty caliber machine gun shells are exploding and the wreckage is giving off a big column of black smoke. Yet, the farmer seems to take no notice. (Robert comes to understand later, as he reflects, that with German soldiers nearby, the farmer doesn't dare get involved.)

As he glances skyward, Robert sees two or three chutes still coming down, in the distance. This gives him heart that maybe all got out in time. Bombs are exploding nearby as other formations of B-26's are bombing the same target. But where to hide in this big open field? As he balls the chute up to avoid detection he sees what appears to be a wheat field on the other side of a nearby road. He runs for it, stopping once to remove his Mae West life preserver. A truck is coming as he crosses the road and runs into the field. He ducks down into the waist high cover. The truck roars up and Robert peeks up to see several German soldiers lining up across the field. As they advance into the field in a plan to flush him from cover, he makes an almost fatal mistake of peeking up again and ducking back down. This poor maneuver brought them all into firing position from about fifty yards. Looking down five gun barrels gives Robert a feeling he is about

SHOT DOWN

Our Robert was shot down over Chartres, France, May 26, 1944, in this plane, (KS-S) B-26 Martin Marauder, on his 60th mission. Of the six man crew, three were killed. This was a relatively new plane on its 14th mission. The right engine was blown off by flak from a German 88 M.M. gun. The left engine was knocked out of commission and the controls jammed. Chutes were seen to open. Robert was the pilot.

I NEVER GAVE UP

Details finally came to us through the proper channels. We kept the faith and flew this beautiful flag for him in our front yard. Our prayers were finally answered after many distressful days and nights.

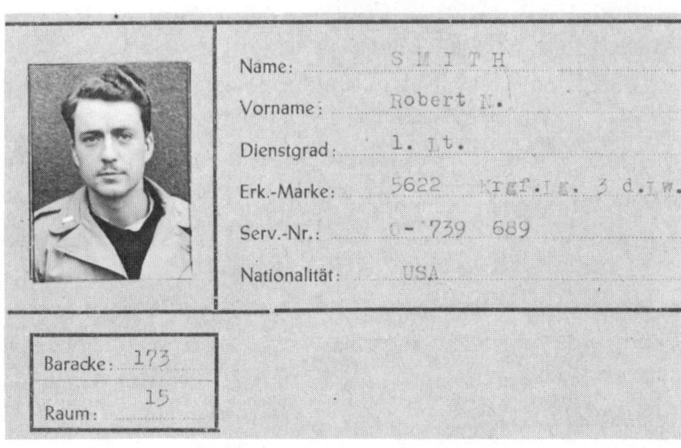

Name: S M I T H

Vorname: Robert N.

Dienstgrad: 1. Lt.

Erk.-Marke: 5622   Krgf.Lg. 3 d.Lw.

Serv.-Nr.:   O-739 689

Nationalität: USA

Baracke: 173

Raum: 15

INTERESTING SOUVENIR

Robert's prisoner identification was recovered from a German file after Hitler's forces surrendered. It was forwarded to Robert by the War Department after he was discharged.

to be executed. He raises his hands in surrender and hopes no one has an itchy finger. Fortunately for Robert, they were not the young Hitler trained SS troops or he would have been shot on the spot.

Instead he was searched and taken to a nearby gestapo headquarters where he was questioned then placed in an old bug infested prison cell. There, alone with his thoughts, he ponders what the Germans will do with him next. He has a few minor cuts and scrapes but is otherwise uninjured. His thoughts turn again to his crew. Had they all got out in time? Was anyone injured? He would find out later that three were killed but under what circumstances he does not know to this day. There were rumors that some were shot in their parachutes as they drifted into the target area. Robert feels that delay in freeing himself from the planes bombay, the delay in opening his chute, and a fast free fall to the ground prevented him from drifting into the target area and saved his life. (Robert and Charles Wright, the Bombardier, had a joyful reunion six months later in the prison camp. Charles had originally escaped and was with the French underground for a short time, only to be picked up by the Germans in Paris.)

Co-pilot Neil Bartholomew was reported alive but all efforts to locate him since the war have failed.

After his capture, Robert was processed through an interrogation center then several detainment camps. He eventually arrived at Stalag Luft III located at Sagan in lower Silesia, ninety miles southeast of Berlin and seventy-five miles northwest of Breslau.

The name Stalag Luft III will long be remembered by thousands of America's flying men. They had flown into action over Europe's war-stricken land, met the enemy and were to remain prisoners of war of the German Luftwaffe for the duration. The prisoners were known as "Kriegies", a contraction of the German word "Kreigsgefangenen," meaning prisoners of war. There were over 10,000 "Kriegies" (POW's) confined in the several camps making up Stalag Luft III.

Life in the camp was hectic with the crowded conditions, shortage of food and clothing, and the ever presence of fleas, bedbugs and lice. Robert, as a child, was the neatest of my boys. He was accustomed to keeping himself clean and well dressed.

However, for the entire year he spent as a German prisoner he had and wore only one pair of pants. He could wash them only when he could borrow an extra pair which circulated among the prisoners for that exclusive purpose. Many a night, he tells me, he spent picking through his clothes in search of crawling and biting insects that prevented him from getting to sleep. Twice a day, morning and night, they were lined up and counted. They had to improvise with what they had in order to survive mentally and physically. Things seemed pretty rough but the worst was yet to come.

In January, 1945 the Russian armies were advancing on the eastern front and threatened to overrun the camp. The Germans were determined, at all cost, not to allow the captive airmen to fall into Russian hands and ordered the evacuation of the camp at 8:30 P.M. on January 27, 1945, giving them one hour to be ready to move.

Having heard rumors of such a move, each man had fashioned a makeshift pack or in some cases a sled made from whatever scraps of lumber he could scavenge. Robert had fashioned a backpack made from an old shirt buttoned up and with the bottom folded up and pinned securely. The sleeve-ends were then tied together with a piece of rope and the arms then served as a harness over the shoulders. In this pack he carried a blanket and personal items along with a Red Cross food parcel issued before the start of the march. This pack was to cause Robert quite a bit of discomfort. He had recently broken his collar bone in a fall at the camp.

With Russian heavy artillery fire heard audibly from the east, the prisoners reluctantly moved out at midnight heading southwest into the face of a full blown blizzard. It was a despairing ten thousand or more men who walked out into the blizzard that night away from the hope sounding in the east. They will forever remember the tortuous trek that followed into the ever increasing fury of the blizzard. Snow fell for four days in sub-zero temperatures, making the progress extremely difficult. Blisters, frozen feet and hands and sickness all contributed to the misery of the exhausted prisoners headed for some undisclosed destination beyond the reach of the advancing Russian armies. Already in a weakened condition, both mentally and physically, from lack of nutritious food, warm clothing and proper medical attention, they were in no shape to survive the severe environment they were forced to endure. There were many acts of kindness and brotherly love along the way, Robert said. Those who tried to lie down in the snow and give in to exhaustion and freezing were forced to their feet by others to keep them moving. Many grew so weary they discarded everything they carried to keep going.

Little detail is remembered by most of the marchers as they moved along in a dazed and exhausted condition. Occasionally, gun shots could be heard to quell some disturbance somewhere along the endless column. The weather was relentless with snow laden wind and bone chilling temperatures.

After twelve hours of marching with infrequent ten minute rest periods, Robert's group reached Freiwaldau at noon, January 28th for a five hour layover. Freiwaldau provided some shelter in concentration camp buildings but there was insufficient room so groups took turns warming themselves while others waited in the blizzard.

The marching began again that day at 5 P.M. and continued through the night and into the next day, arriving at Muskau shortly after noon, January 29th.

NOTE: An account of this forced march was written after the war by POW Joe Klaus entitled "Maybe I'm Dead", and published by Dell Publishing Company in 1955. It was described as, "The epic story of a forced march made at forty below zero by ten thousand American POW's in the final desperate months of World War II."

Robert recalls walking the final distance to Muskau with another prisoner, and supported between them another dazed and weary POW who had given up.

Having been without sleep now for 54 hours and walked a total of 70 kilometers, the prisoners were too exhausted to go any further. Robert's group found shelter in an old pottery factory where they all slumped onto the floor to get some much needed rest.

Those in his group, who were able, left Muskau the next day, January 30th at 12:30 P.M., and marched on about 18 kilometers, then spent the night in a barn. The next day the group arrived at Spremberg at 11:00 A.M. after a seven kilometer walk with the weather taking a turn for the better. There they were given their first hot food, a bowl of barley gruel, and it sure tasted good. They were then moved to the freight yards, a distance of approximately 4 kilometers and placed in box cars.

While this was to mark the end of the marching, it wasn't by any means the end of the misery that still was ahead. They had covered a distance of approximately 100 kilometers (62 miles) in less than four days under the most trying conditions. There were thousands still coming behind with the column spread out and stretching for miles. Many men were missing and never were accounted for.

Forty and eight French freight cars were used to transport the prisoners the rest of the way. (Forty and eight was a French measure of capacity meaning that these small box cars would hold forty men or eight horses.) While affording some protection from the elements, the fifty prisoners and one German guard were packed in so tight that there was barely room for all to sit down. With many sick and all in an exhausted condition, sanitation became a real problem on this trip. While the train would stop occasionally, a single can and hole in the side of the box car served mainly as their latrine. The trip to Moosburg, in southern Germany, took several days with many sidetracks to let other trains pass and mostly night travel to avoid detection from American fighter planes. One day they were mistaken as a supply train and strafed by American fighters. Some casualties were reported but none in Robert's box car.

Their final destination, in southern Germany, was Stalag VII A located at Moosburg near Munich and approximately thirty miles from the ill-famed Dachau Concentration Camp. There, they were herded together with thousands of other prisoners, moved from all over Germany in the face of the advancing allied forces. Conditions in this extremely overcrowded camp were worse than Stalag Luft III. Along with the bugs, food shortage and dysentary, respiratory problems were prevalent throughout the camp. Sanitation was a real problem with so many crowded together. No fuel was provided for the wood stoves in the unheated buildings thus forcing the prisoners to burn their own bed frames and slats to keep from freezing to death. Also, they removed support beams and boards, very discretely, from the buildings that were sheltering them to burn for heat.

To avoid the overcrowded and filthy buildings, some prisoners, including Robert, moved outside in early April to sleep on the ground when weather permitted.

The Germans were ill equipped to provide for the most basic needs of these men, some of whom had been prisoners for over five years. All the nations fighting together to defeat Hitler's war machine and Nazi Regime were represented.

Hitler was determined to hold them hostage until the end. It was rumored after the war that one of Hitler's last orders was to execute all prisoners but the German high command had lost faith in Hitler and would not carry it out. They knew the end of the Nazi Regime was near.

The German forces continued to crumble under the ground and air assaults by Allied forces and on April 29, 1945 Stalag VII A was finally liberated. The relentless 14th armored division of General George Patton's 3rd Army spearheaded in from the northwest and steamrollered through the area. The long awaited liberation was at hand. Robert recalls this day as one of the happiest in his life; a free man again after almost a year (331 days) in Hitler's Nazi prisoner of war camps.

Events leading up to the liberation started approximately one week earlier when artillery fire became audible from the north. At first it could only be heard in the quiet of the night. Hope was sounding in the air again, but packs were again prepared as it was rumored that another march was imminent and would take them deep into the mountain retreats of southern Germany.

As the artillery fire grew louder, air activities around the camp increased with American fighters (P-51 Mustangs and P-47 Thunderbolts) becoming more active in the area. Air raid attacks were made on Munich to the south and other targets nearby. Medium bomber attacks by B-26 Marauders were made on all sides. The German ME-109 Messerschmitt and FW-190 Focke-Wulf fighters, normally seen every day had disappeared. Two tiny LC-5 planes circled overhead during the day spotting and directing artillery shells pouring into the surrounding area. They would occasionally buzz the camp and "waggle" their wings to the shouting and wildly waving "kriegies." They did an excellent job of spotting since no artillery shells fell within the camp area.

Sunday, April 29 dawned and the air was tense with excitement. As early morning worship services ended two P-51 fighter planes buzzed the camp. A tank was spotted on a hill two or three miles away pouring shells into nearby Moosburg. Soon after, the clatter of machine guns and rifle fire could be heard and the prisoners knew their boys were coming. Bullets whistled through the camp and everyone layed low for the next few hours as the action continued in the surrounding area. There were a few casualties in the camp but none were reported serious. Shortly after noon the German resistance ceased and Moosburg fell. It was a beautiful sight to see the "Stars and Stripes" rising over Moosburg on the church steeple at 12:40 P.M.

First to arrive at the camp was an American tank that crashed through the double ten foot high wire fence and into the camp amidst the scene of the wildest rejoicing one can imagine. Tears of joy were streaming down everyone's face. "Kriegies" climbed onto the tank and embraced the tank commander. Other tanks and armored vehicles soon arrived and proceeded slowly through the camp to the shouts and praises of the deliriously happy prisoners.

A short time later, General Patton came into the American camp to meet a thunderous ovation accorded him by 30,000 POW's. The supremely grateful prisoners climbed onto every vantage point to see and cheer their liberator. Records substantiate that the Moosburg Prison contained 110,000 captives of all nationalities. After the joy and confusion of the liberation subsided, the majority of the ex-prisoners were trucked to Landshut, about ten miles to the northeast and flown from there in C-47 Transports to France to go through processing camps before departure by boat to the United States.

On June 2nd, thirty-four days after liberation, Robert was aboard the troop ship U.S.S. General G. O. Souer, filled with ex-POW's and heading for home.

On June 12, after ten days at sea, they watched through misty eyes in revered silence as the statue of liberty loomed into view through the haze. As Robert described, words could never express the feelings of joy and gratitude he felt to look upon this

A DECORATED HERO

This photograph of Lieut. Smith was taken in England shortly before he was shot down as reported in the local papers. He was the recipient of the Distinguished Flying Cross and eleven Air Medals for his combat missions in Europe during World War II againt the forces of Hitler.

THE THIN MAN

Lieut. Robert Smith and his wife, Beth, after he gained back twenty pounds in France and aboard ship before arriving in the United States. As his mother, I cannot visualize how thin he must have been as a prisoner.

symbol of freedom after two years of war and prison camp. Those, like Robert, who were still sound in body and mind felt most fortunate and thankful to return to this wonderful country of ours to start life anew. They were proud to be Americans and glad to be home.

A great price was paid for this freedom by those who gave their lives, and those who will still suffer from their physical and mental scars for the rest of their lives. To these men, we are eternally indebted for their great sacrifice in the name of freedom.

The Red Cross will forever be remembered with gratitude for their indispensable services rendered during the hectic days of internment in the Reich. Without question, many of the returning men would not have survived without the food parcels and other services and intervention rendered by the Red Cross.

For his service to his country during World War II, Robert was awarded the Distinguished Flying Cross and eleven air medals (air medal with two silver oak leaf clusters). Official word of Robert's liberation came again by telegram from the war department.

It was a glorious day when we knew he was coming home. He had lost forty pounds during the ordeal but was fed and cared for so good on the way home that he had regained some of his weight. We met him at the train in Flint (Beth had gone to Chicago to meet him). There he was, coming down the steps with his overseas cap tilted on the side of his head. As he stepped down we threw our arms around him. The conductor smiled and said, "Make way for the passengers, please," but we were too happy to comply at once.

After Bid received his basic training, he was transferred to a base in the Mojave Desert where he received training as a parachute rigger. While in the parachute loft one day, a Marine fighter pilot hobbled in on crutches looking for Sgt. Smith. The pilot extended his hand and stated "I want to shake your hand, I owe my life to you. The parachute you packed for me opened right on time." The pilot had bailed out of his burning fighter plane, landing in the rough terrain in the mountains breaking his leg.

Helen had joined Bid in Mojave for a few months when it was learned he would be going overseas soon. He returned home for a short goodby visit and left for overseas. It was a tearful parting. He was assigned to the Asiatic/Pacific Theatre of Operations, serving on the island of Guam in the Mariana Islands. His letters came and how we did enjoy them. They were always signed "Love and Kisses." He seemed so young and we missed him so much.

During his tour of duty in the Pacific, Bid's unit participated in the battles of Okinawa and Iwo Jima, resupplying the troops and evacuating the wounded. The Japanese suffered heavy losses in the Pacific and on August 6, 1945, the atomic bomb was dropped on Hiroshima followed by another one on Nagasaki on August 9, 1945, forcing the Japanese government to surrender to General Douglas McArthur on August 15, 1945. Bid was with the Occupational Forces that landed in Japan soon after the surrender.

In December of 1945, Victor, Jr. returned home after three years service. When he arrived, we were all waiting for him at

OUR MATURED FAMILY

We gave, each in our own way and according to our ability, all we could to our nation in the war effort. Our home, our jobs, our business and nearly, in some instances, our lives. God has been good and watched over us. In return, we have received some fine daughter-in-laws and grandchildren.

OLD MARKER REPLACED

At my parents grave site in the Fairview Cemetery, Linden, Michigan with my namesake Justine Ann. Their stone has just been replaced with this sparkling new marker.

the train station. He looked so handsome in his Marine uniform. He didn't seem to see us at first, his eyes were on sweet little Cathy Jean, his first born, whom he had never seen. He soon had her in his arms loving her.

When the war ended, Vernon had completed his pilot training so he was a Lieutenant, also, could fly many types of planes and was ready to go overseas. He had served as an instructor pilot training others to fly the biggest four engine bombers of that time (B-24's and B-29's). What a rejoicing when the ordeal was finally over, all three boys were home and we could all settle down to our daily routine. We were proud of our three boys for what they had done for our country.

With the rejoicing after the war also came a sad note. In August of 1945 Pa died, nine years after my mother. He would have been 87 in October of that year.

CHAPTER XIII

RETURN TO NORMALCY

WORLD WAR II played havoc with our family. It came at a crucial time when Vic and I were in our prime years and when our boys were making plans to further their education and careers. It was disruptive but not fatal. We coped, lived in it, through it and survived. All my prayers were answered in the affirmative except for a trio of accidents which none of us anticipated.

Thus this terrible war served as a benchmark in my life. Everything that happened was either before or after World War II, even though as a young woman I suffered the effects of World War I.

Son Robert had worked at the A.C. Spark Plug Division of General Motors before going into the service so they kept his job for him. Before being mustered out he was promoted to the rank of Captain. He enrolled at the General Motors Institute under a cooperative Engineering Program. Robert graduated from G.M.I. in 1950 with a Bachelors Degree in Industrial Engineering with honors and a membership in the Tau Beta Pi Association. This is the national organization for distinguished engineering scholars. He continued his employment at A.C., advancing

ROBERT AND FAMILY

Robert and Beth enjoyed a good life together and raised three fine sons. Standing from left, Richard and Ronald. Fond memories of Robert Jr. (in picture) live on in a special way to each of them.

through several managerial positions until retirement in 1980 as Manager of Projects and Work Orders.

Robert and his devoted wife Beth celebrated their 44th wedding anniversary on March 9, 1987. They raised three fine grandsons for me, Robert Jr., Richard G. and Ronald B. It was a tragic blow to them to lose Robert Jr. in an auto accident in 1970. Richard became a scholar earning Bachelors, Masters and Doctoral Degrees in Psychology. He served for ten years at the Kalamazoo Psychiatric Hospital advancing to the position of Divisional Director of the Psychological Department. To further broaden his experience and desires for the future, he transferred to the Michigan State Police in Lansing where he is now provid-

AT THE ZENITH OF HIS CAREER

Victor H. Smith, Jr. (Bid, to me) became the most well known of any of my boys. I have made several large scrap books of his exploits. There was some talk of his becoming a candidate for Sheriff of Genesee County, but he never got around to doing anything about it.

ing psychological services for State Police personnel, including their families. Ronald, their third son, currently works at A.C. as a plastics injection molding machine operator. After taking courses at Flint Junior College, Ronald decided employment at A.C. was more to his liking where his dad had worked for forty years. Both Richard and Ronald are avid sportsmen with a great love for the outdoors. I am certain they take after me. They and

FLINT PISTOL TEAM

L to R: William Boudreau, Patrolman; Charles Crawford, Detective; Victor Smith, Detective Sargent; Robert Corrington, Captain. Teams which included my son Victor always brought back their share of trophies.

ON INDIANA UNIVERSITY COMBAT RANGE,
BLOOMINGTON, INDIANA

L to R: Charles Crawford, Detective; Victor, Jr., Detective Sgt.; James Bourke, Detective and John R. Burton, Lieutenant.

their father Robert have enjoyed many hunting trips together in Michigan, Colorado and Wyoming.

In 1947 Victor, Jr. was appointed as a patrolman in the Flint Police Department. My, was I proud. When the Korean War broke out in 1950 he was recalled to active duty with the Marines. It was rough. He had to leave little Cathy Jean and Thomas Henry. After several months, Helen and the children joined him in North Carolina at Camp Lejeune.

While at Camp LeJeune Cathy Jean suffered a ruptured appendix. She was critical. I just got in the car, took little Cathy's Aunt Carrie and we drove straight through to that hospital in North Carolina. I went in and asked a nurse if Cathy Smith was still alive. They said she was but just barely. After several touch and go days she began to improve. We were so thankful. She was

WINNERS WITH THE CHIEF

L to R: George B. Paul, Chief of Police; Victor H. Smith, Jr., Detective Sgt.; Charles Crawford, Detective; John R. Burton, Lieutenant (Flint Police Training Office and, later, Chief of Police); Bruce Harbin, Detective.

the only child in the military hospital and everyone was very happy when the word was out that she was going to make it.

Little Justina Ann, my namesake, was born while Victor, Jr. was on this tour of duty.

Victor, Jr. was honorably discharged as a Staff Sergeant in December, 1951, and returned to the Flint Police Department. Victor, Jr. has always liked law enforcement. Because of his intel-

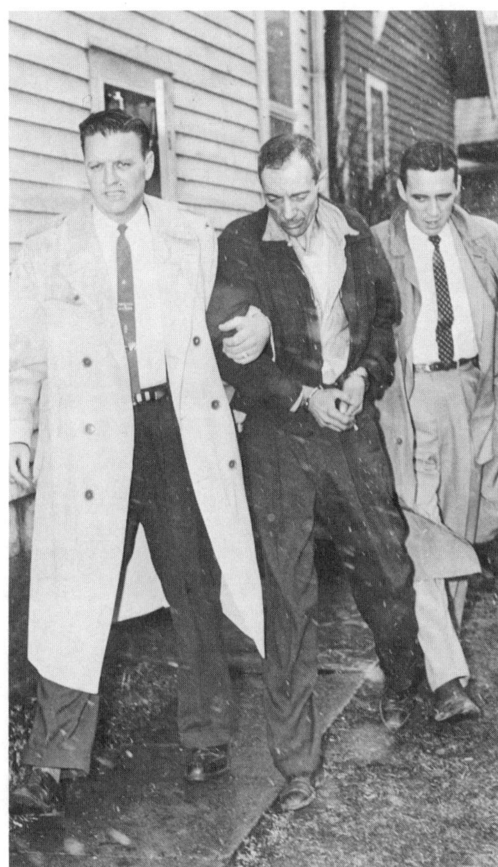

AFTER THE SHOOT-OUT

Detective Sargent Victor Smith apprehending bank robber George Ballin, assisted by F.B.I. Special Agent Martin McNerney. Ballin was flushed from a garage behind 3402 Lewis St. after a gunfight on Saturday, April 7, 1956. He had robbed the Citizen's Bank at the corner of Lewis and East Hamilton Streets Friday morning and escaped with $63,204.00. The money was recovered. Ballin received a lengthy sentence for the robbery and assault on my son Victor with a firearm. He died in prison.

ligence, athletic ability and physical stature, he was a natural for the police department. Before long he was promoted to the rank of Detective.

Through his firearms training in the Marine Corps., and the training with the police department, he became a "Master" Marksman with the pistol and won many honors in both team and individual competition. These awards were on local, state and national levels. There was scarcely a day went by that his name or picture would not appear in the newspaper. In 1955, then Vice-President Richard M. Nixon and his wife, Pat, visited

A NATIONAL AWARD

J. Edgar Hoover looks up to Bid, the number one sharpshooter, on October 31, 1966. The photograph was taken in front of Mr. Hoover's desk in his office at the Justice Building, Washington, D.C. L to R: Victor, Jr., Lieutenant, Flint Police Department; J. Edgar Hoover, Director, F.B.I.; Joseph Casper, Ass't Director, F.B.I.

VICTOR JR., AND FAMILY

Victor Jr., with wife Shirley and daughters, bottom left to right, Pamela, Justine and Catherine. Pamela has red hair like mine and Justine (Tina) is my namesake.

Flint. Victor, Jr. was assigned as their personal bodyguard and chauffeur. As a result of this service, Victor, Jr. received a personal letter of appreciation from Vice-President Nixon.

Over the ensuing years, he was involved in many arrests, trials and convictions of criminals, too numerous to mention. I kept a large scrapbook of news articles of his activities for several years. It measures 25" × 20" and is about 4" thick. It could be called "A Criminal History of Flint." Here are just a few samples of the headlines contained in the scrapbook:

"Fifty-five Ask for Hearings in Liquor Raid"
"Two Cops Decorated for Valor, with Huge Cake"
"Broadway Fire Set, Man Seized for Questioning"

CAPTAIN SMITH'S BADGE RETIRED

After 27 years service. With his wife Shirley at his side, Captain Smith passes the reins to Detective Thomas Smith who follows in his father's footsteps with the Flint Police Department — life and our family goes on and I am proud of them all.

"$2,000.00 Stolen from Kosher Market, Youth Arrested"
"Fugitive Tries To Flee in Police Car"
"Woman Slashes City Detective" (my boy)
"Youth Halted By Shot"
"Two Jail Breakers Caught"

And so it continued.

These newspaper accounts of Victor, Jr's. work goes on for pages. I hope someone takes care of this scrapbook. Someday it will be valuable. Maybe it should be given to a museum; perhaps they do not want to remember this seedy side of Flint.

The Flint News-Advertiser had a columnist, Eldred Lee Miller, who about once a week wrote "Along The Police Beat." Without anyone's permission I would like to reproduce a portion of one of his columns right at this point in my autobiography. I do not even know what date it was published. Maybe some reader will know.

ALONG THE POLICE BEAT with Eldred Lee Miller
News-Advertiser Police Reporter, Flint, Michigan
"There's a couple of slick operators in the Detective bureau known as the "Smith Brothers," Vic Smith and Bob Smith (no relation) who can spot a phony story a mile away.

In the space of a few days recently they took three men into Municipal court on charges of making false reports. All paid fines or served jail terms. You know, it's against the law to make a false report to police.

Just last week Vic, working alone, wormed an admission from a fourth man that the weird tale he had told police had been concocted out of his own mind.

Funny thing how these two guys can smell those whoppers. The innocent bystander would read over those fabrications and accept them at their face value. Might even shed a mental tear for the poor fellow who has been "assaulted and robbed," or "whose wife had attempted to poison him."

But not Vic and Bob. They'll scan the typewritten report and then announce briefly, "Here's another one."

Now remember, 99.4 per cent of the reports taken at police headquarters are on the up and up. So you can see how handy it is to have a couple of boys like Bob and Vic Smith around to sift the wheat from the chaff, so to speak.

The thing of it is, they never get tough with those perpetrators of lies which are a trifle shadier than white. Nope, they just work along deftly and smoothly and wring a confession before the fellow even realizes he is making one.

Fact is, they sort of apologize, and tell the guy how sorry they are that they have to take him into court. Then they explain, patiently, too, that he has wasted many hours of their time investigating his trumped-up story.

The detective bureau is always behind on its investigations. It is swamped. The hours they spent might well have been used on a legitimate complaint.

They wind up by chiding the man for wasting the taxpayer's money. They often end up with having the fellow feeling sorry for Vic and Bob Smith. And that takes the type of diplomacy which often is lacking in the capital of the U.S.of A.

Why do folks make up these myths and then run to police with a heart-rending tale of abuse and robbery, and the like? Well, there's a reason, and that is generally to cover up something they don't want someone else to know about. They figure if they make a report to police, it will remove suspicion of some misbehavior. Heavens, if the family ever found out.

Here's a sample of what might actually have happened— though I confess I'm making the thing up out of whole cloth. No, officer, this is not a formal complaint.

A guy gets out of work off the second shift. It's pay night and it's been a hard week. He feels like kicking up his heels. Could be he spots a dolly who intimates he's the apple of her eye.

She's after entertainment, so is he. The legitimate drinking places are closed. So, flattered by her attentions, they visit places which do not quite conform to the rules.

Drinks are more expensive. Maybe there's some gambling. In one way or another he finally ends up much the worse for wear financially and physically.

Now it's time to repent, time to go home. Listen, would you tell your wife the truth? Well, that's what those other guys do, too. They go to headquarters and report they were held up and robbed.

You can't help pitying the fellows who get all fouled up and then get caught at it.

TRADE AND MARK

Detectives Victor Smith and Robert Smith, no relation, who work as a team have earned a couple of added nicknames. Some of the fellow dicks refer to them as the Smith Brothers and others as "Trade" and "Mark."

I was always concerned about Victor, Jr's. physical safety while he was fighting crime. However, one time I was very concerned about a political reprisal against him when he implicated a strong political figure in a bribery case. That was in January of 1957 when he became mixed up in the Jake Waldo case. A Flint racketeer, James Barraco and a group of other hoodlums got to running, or trying to control, Flint and Genesee County. Waldo appeared on the surface to be a politician but the whole bunch were nothing but gangsters. Waldo was a leader in Democratic politics, head of the UAW-CIO Political Action Committee and had attempted to bribe Victor to lay off some of his gambling dens. He was convicted with the assistance of Vic's testimony. These were not ordinary criminals. God must have been watching over my boy.

In 1966, Victor, Jr. was appointed by the Chief of Police to attend the 78th session of the F.B.I. National Academy in Washington, D.C. This was an honor and privilege as he joined the ranks of only 5,000 graduates from around the world who had graduated from this prestigious institution since its inception in 1935.

While in attendance, Victor, Jr. won the "American Legion National Academy Firearms Proficiency Award," and the "F.B.I. National Academy (Possible Club) Award." Both awards were presented to Victor, Jr. by J. Edgar Hoover, Director of the F.B.I. Victor, Jr's. name has permanently been inscribed in the archives of the F.B.I. National Academy at the Marine Corp. Base in Quantico, Virginia for his firearms exploits on the combat range.

In 1971 Victor, Jr. was called upon by the F.B.I. Training Division to author an article "The Safety of The Police Weapon in the Home." This article was published in the F.B.I. Bulletin and distributed world wide to all law enforcement communities.

During Victor, Jr's. law enforcement career, he encountered many life-threatening situations but always came out unscathed. His closest encounter with death was a close-quarter gun battle with a notorious bank robber and being slashed with a knife by a prostitute while arresting her.

Victor, Jr. has received many departmental citations and commendations for outstanding police work and is the recipient of the "Meritorious Citation" for action above and beyond the call of duty.

The north end of the City of Flint was the most notorious area for crime and a considerable amount of Vic, Jr's. time was spent there. He was respected and the people in the area nick-named him "The Viking." When "The Viking" was on the street word went out, and the hoodlums toed the line.

Victor, Jr. was always a credit to the Flint Police Department, and earned the respect of his peers for his honesty, integrity and unselfish devotion to duty. Proud of my boy? You bet I was!

Victor, Jr. rose to the rank of captain and was the commanding officer of the Criminal Investigation Bureau, retiring form the Police Department in July 1974. He then was appointed to the staff of the Genesee County Prosecutors Office as an Investigator, finally retiring in 1978. His son, Thomas Henry, has followed in his father's footsteps and is now a Detective Sergeant in the Criminal Investigations Bureau of the Flint Police Department.

In 1945 Lieut. Vernon Smith was honorably discharged from the Air Force after World War II and returned to civilian life with his wife, Mary, and little Gary Paul.

Vernon wrote the civil service examination for appointment to the Flint Fire Department and placed #1 on the eligibility list. It was learned that his score on the examination was one of the highest ever recorded.

In November 1948 Vernon was appointed a fireman and he quickly advanced to the rank of Sergeant with service at stations #1 and #5 during his career. The majority of his service was at station #5 at Davison Road and Minnesota Avenue right behind our Broadway Street home and our little grocery store on Minnesota.

Vernon was considered a "man's man," and possessed those qualities of intelligence and leadership abilities that made him a

OUR FLINT FIREFIGHTER

Our eldest boy, Vernon, after returning from World War II, was a Flint Fireman. He served with distinction from Stations No. 1 and 5. I am sorry that there is not as much about Vernon to relate to you as there is of the other two boys. He was cut down in the prime of his life. Pa and I did not think we could live through it — but we did.

THE SMITH BROTHERS

Vernon would have been proud of his handsome sons. Michael, second from the left, is the last one to get married. His brothers from the left are Gary, best man Vernon Jr., and Gordon.

natural supervisor. It was learned that Vernon would be the first firefighter at the scene to enter a building raging with fire where others would hesitate to go. One fire in particular was related to me. Vernon and his crew responded to a fire that occurred at the Phillip "66" Bulk storage yard located at Longway Boulevard and Kearsley Park. A long storage warehouse, right next to gasoline storage tanks in the yard, was being consumed by fire. Firemen at the scene related that Vernon, without hesitation, was the first to don his oxygen mask, pick up a three inch fire hose and disappear into the intense heat, smoke and fire. He never expected the men under his command to enter where he dared not go. Yes, Vernon was like that. He was intensely loyal to his friends and very protective of his younger brothers, Bob and Vic.

Vernon seemed to possess innate teaching abilities and because of his expertise and in-depth knowledge of fire fighting tactics, he also served as an instructor in the Flint Fire Department Training Academy.

During the ensuing years, Vernon and Mary were blessed with 3 more handsome sons; Vernon John, Jr., Gordon Murray and Michael Rudolph.

Although Vernon and Mary's marriage ended in divorce, the four boys grew into fine young men, each one of them striving for excellance in his own field of endeavor. I am very proud of each one of them.

Gary studied at General Motors Institute taking courses in management and electrical engineering and is currently employed at Buick as a machine repairman. Vernon, Jr. graduated from the University of Michigan (Flint) with a Bachelor's Degree in applied sciences and industrial management and is employed at Consumers Power Co. as district superientendant for energy services in the Lansing area. Gordon received his bachelor's degree in industrial education from Eastern Michigan University and a Masters Degree in education and administration from the University of Michigan (Flint) and currently is director of vocational education for Genesee County Intermediate School District. Michael is currently studying at University of Michigan (Flint) towards a bachelors degree in applied sciences and industrial management, while, at the same time, working at Consumers Power Co. as supervisor for energy services in the Fenton area.

In addition to the four boys by Mary, Vernon had two additional children; another son Robert Vernon and a daughter Verna Marie by his second wife Velta (Beavers). Verna Marie was born shortly after Vernon's untimely death in 1958 and Velta then took the two children and moved to Kentucky to be near her parents.

She has since remarried but I have managed to stay in close contact with her and my two other grandchildren, Robert and Verna.

While the loss of their father was a great blow to all of us, Vernon's boys have through their own initiative and perseverence obtained an education and risen to a status in life where their father would be extremely proud of them.

After World War II was over, Victor Sr. had gone to work on a salaried job in the blueprint room at the Buick Motor Division. He was in charge of several girls and liked his job very much.

I was still inspecting at the Marvel Carburetor Plant. Why was I doing this uninteresting work when I had a life certificate to teach? I had been out so long, I hesitated to start in again but I had heard of a vacancy at the Wolcott School on South Vassar Road. They needed a 5th and 6th grade teacher, so I applied and got the job. It was a heavy load, but the Kindergarten teacher took some of my classes. I also taught music in all grades through the 8th.

After two years at the Wolcott School, I took another position at the Dye School on Corunna Road at a better salary. This school was better equipped, with a good library, gym and hot lunches. I did enjoy my 6th grade, especially in the art work they did and the programs we put on. One I particularly remember was "Jack and the Beanstalk." I had charge of the costumes, and when we needed a cow I made one of burlap and two children were chosen from my room to be the cow. A set of twins who could step around with comic antics filled the part perfectly. It took the house by storm. I had to take a bow for making the cow look so real, and the twins were applauded for their splendid performance. I stayed at Dye School six years.

In the meantime, I kept up my studies and had credits transferred from Mt. Pleasant to Eastern Michigan University at Ypsilanti, for their classes were available in Flint. I also did some work by correspondence.

About the time I started teaching at the Wolcott School in 1945, we bought some lots at Higgins Lake and had a cottage built from ready-cut lumber from East Tawas. I had fun drawing the blueprints using the scale of one quarter inch to the foot. The lumber was cut accordingly and came out well. This kept me

DYE SCHOOL FACULTY, 1950

L to R, top row: Ruth Burton, Helen Cole, Y. Miller, M. Brockway, C. Schuler, M. Hagemeister, G. Urckman, Lois Habecker. Middle row: Justina Smith, R. Royal, M. Foley, M. Barrett, Mrs. McLaren, C. Cook, Mrs. Roberts, G. Young. Bottom row: J. Randels, Supt., R. Sullivan, M. Teegarden, H. Wilkins, G. Scott, D. Dean, C. Foster — the finest group of teachers I ever worked with.

BENTLY SCHOOL, 6TH GRADE

This was one of my favorite classes — my 6th grade at Bentley, February, 1956.

TEACHING CAREER WINDS DOWN

I resumed teaching after the War. In turn, I taught for two years at Wolcott, six years at Dye and at Bentley until my retirement in the spring of 1957. Photograph was taken with a pair of teacher-quality apples. I was paid and fed well.

JUSTINA E. SMITH, RETIRED

Justina E. Smith, retired before the time of the writing of this book.

busy, along with my teaching and classes; sometimes one right after school and then one at night. I took a lunch along for between classes.

In 1952, we decided to make the Broadway place into a two-apartment dwelling to rent and have a new home built in the East Court Street area. We loved our new home.

The Bentley School was closer, so in 1952 I got a position in grade six and found it better than at Dye, staying there four years.

After attending two summer terms at Eastern Michigan University, I finally received my B.S. degree in 1956. I then taught until my retirement in the spring of 1957.

CHAPTER XIV

OUR RETIREMENT AND THREE TRAGEDIES

NOW THAT I have retired, Victor began making plans for his retirement. That would give us more time at our cottage at beautiful Higgins Lake. It was especially beautiful there in the fall of 1957. The gorgeous colors of red and yellow blended with the evergreens. Sunsets were the prettiest and our cottage was situated so we had full benefit of them. The ground was covered with a carpet of red and yellow leaves. These had to be raked up before snow came. It was quite a task, raking long rows and piling them onto a tarpaulin to be dragged back into the woods and spread evenly around. The days grew shorter and each day the sunset a little farther south. Brisk breezes across the lake chilled us to the bone and numbed fingers. When we could no longer grasp our rakes we knew it was time to winterize the cottage by draining all water pipes. This brought thoughts of going to a warm climate. We talked it over and decided even a three week trip would be nice. So we got ready and set out for Florida. This was our first visit there and we visited every place of interest. We even went as far south as Key West, where we bought key lime pie and ate it walking down the street. I have pictures to prove it.

We took a more central route on the way home. When we

HIGGINS LAKE COTTAGE

I liked to go there even in the winter, build a roaring fire in that great fireplace, pop corn and live it up.

arrived on January 7, 1958, we found a note on our back door saying, "Let us know when you arrive." We wondered why such an urgent request. I wanted to get unpacked and freshen up before calling anyone. It was getting toward evening and it would be plenty of time to visit when I had everything in order. We heard steps on the back porch and soon we were greeting Bob and Bid with hugs and kisses. We went to the living room and sat down. We did notice the boys were strangely quiet. At that point, I asked, "Where is Vernon?" I thought he might be on duty at the fire station. "Vernon was in an accident," they said, "and it was fatal." What a crushing blow! Their dad collapsed and we had to have Dr. Dodds come. This had happened while we were on our way home. The police were trying to find us and bring us home. The funeral had been postponed from Tuesday to Friday. The accident happened at a crossing on Coldwater Road on a cold frosty night, January 5th. Two firemen, Vernon and Del Farner were on their way home from a fireman's meeting. Vernon was driving, but never saw or heard that train as it rounded a mound

OLDEST SON VERNON, KILLED

A car-train crash on Coldwater Road at the Chesapeake and Ohio tracks took Vernon from us January 5, 1958. They had to cut him out of the wreckage. Another fireman, Delton Farner, riding with Vernon, was thrown from the car and also killed.

of dirt near the Ternstedt Plant. There was no signal at the crossing, but one was installed after those dear boys met their death. Such sad funerals. Vernon was only 37. Days and years have gone on, but we will never forget our dear, sweet, handsome son.

Because Vernon was cut down while in the prime of life his life story stops here. There was no more to write about him except the following poem which I wrote.

DARLING VERNON'S GRAVE

I stood beside his lonely grave
  As the evening sun sank low
The waning light cast shadows long
  Across the drifted snow.

No sound was there, but whispering winds
  And as my tears were shed
Soft breezes rippled the evergreens
  That blanketed his bed.

My thoughts turned back to yesteryears
  To the carefree days of joy
When I tucked him snugly in his bed
  My darling little boy!

The years rolled on, and he grew strong
  So handsome and so tall
Life held for him such promises
  But so suddenly came his "call."

No more I see his dear sweet face
  Or hear his familiar tread
For the Master's Hand has tucked him in
  To his eternal bed.

Away from earthly grief and care
  Away from toil and pain
But some glad day not far away
  I'll see his face again.

Justina E. Smith

Then Victor retired from Buick, he just couldn't go on. I was glad I had retired just before this happened. Vernon lies at rest in Fairview Cemetery near Linden, where most of my relatives are and where I will be. A veteran's stone is there and each Decoration Day a flag flies over his grave.

Now I had nothing to keep me real busy except my house-

"EVANGEL HOUR FOUR"

Victor and I teamed up with some good friends who were beautiful singers — the Carpenters — to broadcast a radio program over station WMPC in Lapeer, Michigan, each week in 1941.

work and an occasional visit to the cottage. We went to church and sang in the choir. I did a lot of sewing on my little portable. It was a handy machine and I made a lot of clothes; dresses, a suit or two, a white velvet coat and skirt to match and a plaid coat and skirt and hat to match. I also made a brown suit trimmed with braid with a hat to match. I just kept busy, busy. It is my style of life, always has been and perhaps always will be.

Then I bought a Hammond Organ and started to play again. I had a nice Grinnell Piano, but when we moved I turned it in on the organ and only got $75.00 credit. I had bought it years ago and learned to play. It had a lovely tone but the organ did not take up so much room. I also had a guitar I used to strum and sing just for my own amusement. Guess I was "Jack of all trades and Master of none."

After that I took up oil painting. After a few lessons at Mott I loved it. If I had started younger, think I would have done well. My teacher praised my work and, of course, I liked that. I had done crayon work at school and chalk pictures, but I loved the

AT THE HAMMOND

Our new home in the East Court Street area of Flint was the third and last home we owned. Jennie Snyder, a friend, is listening to an old hymn I am playing.

oils. We made a studio up in our attic that was finished off into a nice room, bought paints by the score, frames and canvas and many books showing how to make landscapes, seascapes, etc. In all, I made over thirty-five, some large and some small, mostly landscapes, Arizona scenes from places we had visited and ideas from the Arizona Highway Magazine. Some I gave away to the children who wanted them and some I still have stored. I never sold any for didn't think they were good enough.

In 1964, Victor and I celebrated our 50th wedding anniversary. It was given by our children and their families at the First Wesleyan Church on Davison Road. The church was all newly remodeled and we were the first to celebrate a 50th anniversary in it.

At this point in my life, the grandchildren were taking up much of my time and interest in life. They were graduating from high school and starting college. They were mostly boys, and the youngest one was little Mark, the youngest child of Victor, Jr. and Helen. He was born in 1960, a bright, sweet little fellow. He loved to go up to the cottage and play in the water. He just loved everybody. One Christmas he wanted a guitar and a bicycle. He was only four then, and I have his picture with that small play

TROUBLE IN THE DESERT

What became of the wheels and the driver? I have often wondered about this. I took this picture on one of our trips to Arizona.

guitar. He is holding the doll I have had since I was four, in one arm and in the other he is clutching the Santa Claus I made in one of my classes at Eastern Michigan University. Sitting beside him in that picture is his sister, Pamela, age nine. He was too young for a bike then. Just four years later, when he was eight, he was out playing with Pamela and a neighbor girl, who was twelve. The girls were riding their bikes along Seymour Road. They had been told not to ride double or on a busy road, but it was summer and they were having fun. The morning sun was bathing the flowers in the fields with sunshine. No traffic was in sight and the smooth pavement looked so inviting. Leslie, the twelve year old, put Mark on the bike and started out. Pamela was ahead. As she rounded a slight curve, she saw a car coming and warned Leslie. Pam pulled off on the shoulder, but Leslie tried to make it to the other side. The car struck her while throwing them to the pavement and skidded into the ditch. Leslie was not injured much but little Mark did not move. He was still breathing and was rushed to Hurley Hospital and placed on a machine that kept his heart going. What a shock it was for all of us. For two days we watched over him day and night. They had stitched up a big gash in his leg and one in his scalp. He did not open his eyes, but was still breathing. The third day the doctor said that tests showed no brain reaction and that the machine would only keep his heart going. Victor, Jr. and Helen had been divorced for about four years when this happened. She had married again to Don and Bid had married Shirley. They were lovely people and when this tragedy struck, we were all melted together like one big heartbroken family. The funeral was large, there were two rooms at Brown Funeral Home filled with beautiful flowers. The procession was long and headed by an escort from the Flint Police Department and the Grand Blanc Police. He was laid to rest in Sunset Hills. Later, a stone was placed on his grave with little pine cones carved on the marble. His dad has one placed beside Mark's with the same design of pine cones. Little Mark was sent to us like a little angel, to help us to live better, and then God took him back to grow in His garden of Love to be a strong force to draw us there.

After this happened, I tried to go on with my painting. I knew it was wrong to grieve too much, but I just could not paint like I did. The first picture was a flop, so I sold all my paints, drawing books and equipment when our next door neighbor had a garage sale. I sold quite a few things I did not need anymore, such as books and figurines. Children I had taught at school had given me so many things, there were only a few I could keep.

In going over my books, I found one of my mother's family records — the Sage Family. It had started with David Sage, the first known, from Wales, by that name. He arrived in the United States in 1639 at the age of twelve. It did not mention his parents. That book got me interested in making a genealogy. The family name had a coat-of-arms and was traced to my grandfather's name and date of birth. I started out, not realizing what a big job I had undertaken. I had to write letters to families I knew, and with the help of the book, after two years, I had it all, including a coat-of-arms printed by hand on a large sheet. It showed each family, the date of birth and death, and lined up so a family can trace back to David Sage by following their family lines. Then each family can add a sheet of their own family record to bring it up to date. These charts are reproduced in detail beginning on page 9 of this book.

We made several trips to Arizona and Florida for our win-

GRANDSON MARK'S NEW BIKE

Mark was photographed a short time before he was struck and killed by a car on Seymour Road near Flushing, Michigan. He was the son of Victor, Jr. and Helen. I liked to run my hand over his crew cut.

ters. Arizona is my choice for winter. I love the desert and especially toward spring when the cacti are a riot of color. My sister, Grace, lived in Phoenix so we always landed at her place. (While living there, Grace was a friend of the Goldwaters.)

On one of our trips to Arizona, we went to the rodeo. Victor dressed in his cowboy hat, tie and shirt and I wore my squaw dress (it was green with silver trimming). I also wore my cowboy hat. We looked just like we belonged in the rodeo. What fun! But I don't think we fooled anyone.

On our next trip to Arizona, a few years later, Grace died while we were there. After a funeral service her body was brought back to Michigan for burial in the old family plot in Fairview Cemetery at Linden.

We also went to Florida several times. I loved the water there. It was fun on the beaches, feeding the gulls and wading in the surf. The Gulf was my choice, especially at Clearwater Beach.

On all our trips, Victor was always so patient with me. He didn't like to explore as much as I did, but would always wait patiently in the car.

Working on the genealogy summers at the cottage and going away for the winter took up my time during those two years after Mark's death. But then another tragedy struck. How could we bear any more. We had gone up to the cottage one weekend and Robert and Beth were with us. Their son, Robert Nathan, Jr. was going to join us after he had finished some school work. He was a teacher at Emerson Junior High in Flint. He was 24 years old and had graduated from Central Michigan University at Mt. Pleasant the year before with a degree in teaching. We were so proud of him. He was the oldest of Robert and Beth's three sons (Robert Jr., Richard and Ronald). He had a girlfriend who worked at Charlevoix and he planned on going up early Saturday morning to bring her back to the cottage so that we might meet her. He left early that morning and we waited all day for them, but they didn't come. I went to Mildred's cottage near ours that night so there would be room for them to sleep. I was tired and retired about 10 P.M. Before going to sleep I heard a knock on the door and it was Robert. What was it that made him stand and look at me as though he could not speak? "It's Bobby," he said. "He was in a bad accident with his new Corvette and he is dead." Seems he had gone to get his girlfriend from her place of work at about 5 P.M. and on the way in rounding a curve, his car flipped over. The top was down and he was crushed under it. It had started to burn and a bus happened along and extinguished the fire. What a tragedy! We went back to the cottage and got ready to leave for home that night. It was a large funeral and he was laid to rest at Sunset Hills. His parents were stunned. They still feel the effects of the loss of their first born.

Years went on and we made a few more trips to Florida. We took many slides and movies of these trips and worked hard to keep up our cottage. Victor began to fail faster than I did. He could no longer drag the tarpaulin full of leaves back into the woods. My eyes began to fail and I could not paint the buildings and keep up with things. During the summer of 1973, my eyes got so bad that I could hardly see. The doctor told me that the cataracts in both my eyes would have to be removed. So I went into McLaren Hospital and had it done, both eyes within the ten days I was there. I have never been able to read since that surgery. Other people do. Exactly what happened I do not know.

I have also made scrap books of the trips we have taken together and they included pictures illustrating these trips. Photography was another of my hobbies and I have more than 300 slides and movie rolls. Someday the children and their families might like to look at these. I have made it a habit to write on every picture, the subject and date so that in the dim future there will be few pictures in which the principals and location cannot be identified.

Through the years I have kept too many "things." I still have every letter the boys wrote to us when they were in the service and many of the little things they made in school. That is being too sentimental, but I could not bear to throw them away. They have been my life.

I received my first doll, for Christmas, when I was four. I have given it to my first great-great-grandchild, Amanda, Vernon's first great-grandchild.

We have given the cabin and lots at Higgins Lake to Robert and Victor, dividing them equally. They have fixed them up and they are in excellent condition now.

ROBERT N. SMITH, JR.

My grandson, and son of Robert and Beth, seemed to be following in my footsteps. He was a teacher at Emerson Junior High in Flint. I was proud of him.

REMAINS OF
NEW CORVETTE

Grandson Robert lost his life on August 8, 1970 at the young age of 24. It was a one car accident on a curve of U.S. 31, south of Charlevoix. He was alone and the road was dry. We never knew what caused his death. Mechanical failure, too much speed, swerved to miss an animal?

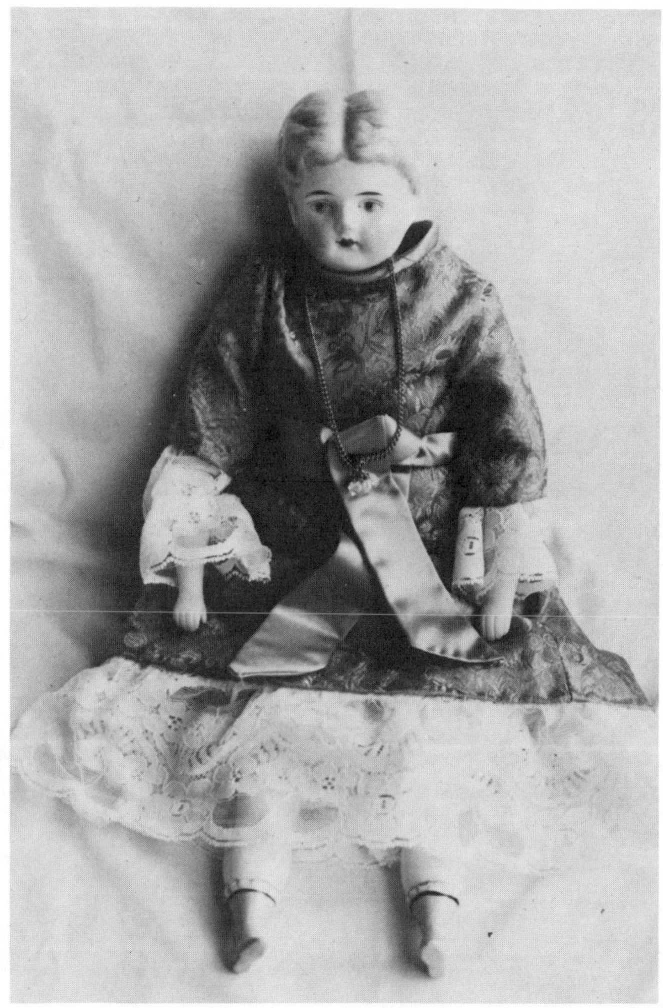

MY DOLL DAISY

This doll first appeared in my Christmas stocking when I was four in 1894. I gave it to my first great-great-granddaughter, Amanda Beverly Smith.

OUR 70TH WEDDING ANNIVERSARY

Friends and relatives gathered at son Robert's home on September 15, 1984 to honor us and brought this huge cake. In spite of my condition, it was a happy occasion.

LAST GOOD PHOTO

Our last good photograph was taken on the porch of our home at 301 South Franklin in Flint when Victor was 90 and I was 92. Above all, he was always a good and faithful husband.

On March 31, 1984. I fell down the steps on the back porch of our home striking the cement walk, breaking my left hip and arm. I was taken to St. Joseph Hospital where a metal plate and pins were inserted into my hip. Then I was released to Briarwood Manor, a nursing home on Center Road, for therapy. When I was here only a short time, I fell again. I am confined to a wheelchair for an indefinite time.

Briarwood has been a blessing to me. It is such a clean place and everyone has been so nice and helpful. They do so much to entertain us and every holiday is remembered with decorations and special meals.

After I came to Briarwood, Victor stayed on at home by himself until my sister, Mary, came and stayed to help him out, for about a year.

CHAPTER XV

THE LIGHTS DIM AND GO OUT

MY LITTLE SISTER, Ruth, died first (after Grace) in July of 1984. She had been living at Higgins Lake, but died in Florida, where she had been spending some time with her daughter, Ann Louise.

One year later my sister, Mildred, passed away here at Briarwood where she had been living.

Then, a few days later, in July of 1985 my husband, Victor, died at home. He would have been 93 on October 31st and we would have celebrated our seventy-first wedding anniversary in September. Victor had been to see me the night before, but when Victor, Jr. went to check on him the next morning (as he or Robert did every day), he found him where he had fallen at the kitchen sink. He had got up, made his bed, fixed his breakfast and was washing the dishes when he collapsed.

Now, Mary and I are the only leaves left on the family tree. She is 90 years old and lives here at Briarwood, also.

Now, as I finish this book in May of 1987, I have two children and twelve grandchildren living, eighteen great-grandchildren and two great-great-grandchildren. Most of my children and grandchildren have attended college. Victor and I have instilled in our family the importance of an education, and

DR. RICHARD G. SMITH

This was my last long trip, unless I get stronger. I went to Kalamazoo to see my grandson receive his Ph.D. in Psychology. He is employed with the Michigan State Police, Lansing.

they have all been interested in that goal. I was so glad to be able to see my grandson, Richard, receive his Doctorate. He is now a Police Psychologist with the Michigan State Police in Lansing.

I am happy to have lived out my life in Michigan, as I wouldn't have wanted to live in any other state. As I said at the beginning of my autobiography, it is truly a WONDERLAND. In the spring it is a green Wonderland, in the summer it is a Water Wonderland with the Great Lakes (also Michigan boasts of over 3000 flowing wells), in the fall a spectacular Wonderland of color and in the winter a white Wonderland. And they are all beautiful.

One of the reasons for writing this book, is to help young people start out right in life. The way is to make up their minds to do what is right and not just go along with the crowd. Listen to what God tells you and put your faith and life in His hands. He is

ENJOYING MY GREAT-GRANDDAUGHTER

Sarah, as she teaches me to play hand jive. Her mother is Rebecca, daughter of Richard Smith, son of Robert. We make a good pair.

always there to help you. Also, listen to your parents and obey and love them.

Hopefully, too, people have found something in my book that will teach them to be kind to animals and appreciate them. They were put on this earth to help us and be companions to us. Children should be taught to treat their pets kindly.

First and foremost, though, is to follow God's teachings for a rewarding, long, happy and healthy life.

MY FIRST GREAT-GREAT-GRANDDAUGHTER

Amanda Beverly, who was brought to see me by her mother, Chris Ann, daughter of Gary Smith, son of my fire-fighting son, Vernon, who left us so young. Having these fine girls about me is refreshing after being overrun with boys most of my life.

MY SECOND GREAT-GREAT-GRANDDAUGHTER

Ashley Nicole, on her 1st visit to see grandma. Feb. 10, 1987. Brought to me by her mother, Sherry Lynn, daughter of Cathy Jean, daughter of my son Victor, Jr.

"GUSSIED" UP FOR A SUNDAY DRIVE

With my sharpshooter Victor (Bid). I called him my personal body-guard — and there was never a better one because he was my son.

GOING TO DINNER WITH BOB

The event was my 97th birthday. We went to Bill Knapps Restaurant. My sister, Mary, and daughter-in-law, Beth, were both with us. The discount on my diinner was 97% — it cost only 30¢. This was January 14, 1987 and I had a lot of fun.

EPILOGUE

ON JUNE 1st, 1987 Justina Eliza Smith died quietly in her sleep at the age of 97 years, 4 months and 18 days. I had spent many hours over the last year and a half with Tina while she told me her life story, finishing the story just before she passed away. Her memory, attention to detail and chronological order of events were remarkable for her age.

It was a privilege for me to know and work with Justina Smith. She was a wonderful, talented and intelligent person and a true Christian lady.

JEANETTE L. DAHLGREN

The family of Justina E. Smith would like to express their appreciation and gratitude to Mrs. Jeanette Dahlgren for her assistance and professional help in making this autobiography a reality.

In hearing that Justina desired to write her life story, Mrs. Dahlgren volunteered her services. She spent countless hours between her home and Briarwood Nursing Home gathering and organizing the information and typing the manuscript.

For her selfless interest and devotion in making this book possible, the family is indeed grateful.

SELECTED
VERSE AND POEMS

By

Justina Eliza Smith

WHEN I GO FISHIN'

When I go fishin' do I have fun!
Sitting all day in the boiling sun!
Drinkin' cool water from a big jug,
Swattin' mosquitoes, flies and bugs
My feet are wet and hands all grime,
But I wash and eat when it comes noontime.

A hole in my hat lets in the breeze
While I nibble away on crackers and cheese,
Fish dart to the surface—out goes my bait!
I may get him yet, if I'm not too late!
Jerk goes my pole—my bobber goes under
And up comes that bluegill for a wonder!

Down goes the sun, up comes the breeze,
I pull up anchor with a lusty heave
A crick in my back as I row for shore,
But next day I go right out for more!
When I go fishin' do I have fun!
And I bring in fish when the day is done.

MARCH WIND

March wind hums a roguish tune,
Tosses clouds across the moon,
Rattles branches brown and bare
And makes great blustering everywhere.

A LITTLE SUNBEAM

A little sunbeam came one day
To melt the winter's snow away,
It beamed and beamed with all its might
And chased old March wind out of sight.

SPRING IS COMING

Rain comes a tapping at the flower's door
Wake up! Wake up! and sleep no more!
Put on your dresses — yellow, pink and blue,
Spring is coming, so hurrying, please do!

SPRING IS HERE

All the flowers are waking from their sleep,
Soon the crocus through the ground will peep
Little birds are singing, sky is clear,
All the world is happy, spring is here!

ROBIN'S SONG

Out in the orchard a sweet robin sings,
Cheeralee! Cheeralee! now it is spring
Skies are all blue and it's time to be gay
Cheer up! Cheer up! he warbles away.

GRAND THINGS OF LIFE

There are so many things to make life grand,
There are beauties of nature on every hand.
Fleecy clouds, blue skies, fields of golden grain
Green grass on the hills — the wind, sun and rain.
The rainbow bright that comes after showers
Sparkling dew, busy bees at work in the flowers.
Waving meadows, and happy birds on the wing,
Colored rocks, sifting sands — little crickets that sing.
Waterfalls, crystal lakes and babbling brooks,
Stately trees, winding paths and shady nooks,
Sunset skies, oceans blue with white crested foam
Stars that twinkle at night and a silvery moon
That sheds soft beams on glistening snow,
Rare beauties through seasons that come and go.
A butterfly's wing and a pink sea shell
More wonderful things than tongue can tell.
Yes, God made this beautiful world and hung it in space
But what would it be without a child's smiling face.

Dedicated to my 6th grade class at Bentley School.

OUT IN THE FIELDS

I love to walk on a bright spring day,
When skies are blue and little birds gay
Are singing a happy cheerful tune
Out in the fields in June.

I love to walk on a summer day
Out in the fields where soft breezes play,
Where the grasses wave and the daisies nod
Out in the fields with God.

I love to walk in the Autumn time
When the trees are clothed in colors fine,
Where the soft down floats from the milkweed pod
Out in the fields of God.

I love to walk on a winter day,
When the air is crisp and long sunbeams play
On the sparkling snow at the close of day
These are gifts from the hand of God.